THE DOG'S DRUGSTORE

Richard W. Redding, D.V.M., M.Sc., Ph.D.
and **Myrna L. Papurt,** B.Sc., D.V.M.

Illustrations by Lisa Makarchuk

St. Martin's Paperbacks

THE DOG'S DRUGSTORE

Copyright © 2000 by Richard W. Redding and Myrna L. Papurt.
Illustrations copyright 2000 by Lisa Makarchuk.
Cover photograph by Chris Jones/The Stock Market

ISBN: 0-312-97889-8

Printed in the United States of America

St. Martin's Press hardcover edition / May 2000
St. Martin's Paperbacks edition / August 2001

St. Martin's Paperbacks are published by St. Martin's Press, 175 Fifth Avenue, New York, NY 10010.

10 9 8 7 6 5 4 3 2 1

APR - - 2002

CONTENTS

FOREWORD

—

An informed owner is a dog's best friend.

—

**When can you use over-the-counter drugs
to help your dog?
Which drugs are dangerous or deadly to dogs?
Which drugs are safe?
Which are effective?
Which are useless?
When *must* you consult your veterinarian?**

At some point every concerned dog owner will ask these questions—and in this book, we will help to answer them. When owners are well informed, they can detect many problems that arise in the health of their dogs. They can also treat some minor ailments and can participate effectively in a treatment program prescribed by their veterinarians.

It is human nature to try something for common and seemingly minor health problems before consulting a professional. The huge nonprescription drug industry depends on it. Thousands of nonprescription drugs are sold over-the-counter every day for use in both humans and animals. Dog owners buy and use over-the-counter (OTC) products for a considerable number of their dogs' medical problems, ranging from arthritis to worm infestation. In the majority of cases, these drugs are helpful, or at least not harmful.

If your dog has a medical problem, should you "let nature

take its course"? Treat it yourself with human or animal nonprescription medications? Call your veterinarian? This book is designed to help you make these vital decisions.

However, never think that you can be your own veterinarian just because you have read this book. Unless you are a graduate of an accredited college of veterinary medicine, you cannot be your dog's veterinarian any more successfully than a parent who is not a medical doctor can be her children's pediatrician. If an owner or a parent believes otherwise, their children and their dogs may be in trouble.

USE THIS BOOK WITH CARE!

Three *vital rules* for using nonprescription drugs in the dog:

—

First

Never substitute or delay essential veterinary care by using an OTC drug for a serious problem. If you had the same condition, would you use OTC drugs or go to your own physician? Treat your dog as you would treat yourself.

Second

Use only drugs that are appropriate for use in dogs. Be careful which human drugs you choose. Some drugs used in humans are harmful, even fatal, to dogs. Some drugs that work well in people are entirely ineffective when given to dogs.

Third

Calculate the doses of all drugs with extreme care. Dogs and humans often require different quantities of the same drug. The dose that is appropriate for a human adult or child may be dangerous or ineffective for a dog.

—

INTRODUCTION

MEDICAL CONDITIONS ARE OF SEVERAL TYPES

All medical conditions are not of equal severity or in equal need of treatment.

Conditions that need no treatment

Some medical conditions need not be treated at all. These are conditions that produce no pain, discomfort, or disability to the patient. Many of these conditions are congenital, meaning that puppies are born with them. An example of a congenital condition that does not require veterinary intervention for the health of the dog is mild dental malocclusion. Unless a puppy has a very severe overbite or underbite, it will be able to function throughout its life in an entirely normal fashion.

Certain conditions may be acquired during the course of a dog's life, and while these conditions are not normal, an affected pet dog can function entirely without pain or impairment. An example of such a condition is a "flat" toe caused by damage to the flexor tendon of the digit. The dog with a flat toe can run without pain, even at the moment of the injury.

Some of dogs' medical conditions are entirely cosmetic. If these conditions are treated, it is for the benefit of the owner, not the dog. The puppy with nonsevere malocclusion is an example of this. A pup with this condition does not need expensive orthodontia to enable it to eat properly. If its owner elects to have his pet undergo treatment to correct a moderate overbite or underbite, it is because the owner prefers that his dog have a perfect "smile." In fact, what constitutes a structural fault for one breed of dog may be the required standard for another breed. For example, the bow legs of the English bulldog would be a serious defect in a whippet.

—

Note: A dog that has had its appearance changed by artificial means is disqualified in the show ring both in American Kennel Club and United Kennel Club shows. The exception to this rule is the docking of tails, the cropping of ears, and the removal of dewclaws of breeds in which this surgery is still permitted.

—

Conditions that will disappear without medical treatment

Dogs with certain medical conditions will get well without treatment. For example, a dog with simple diarrhea from overeating will recover in a day or two, just as a person with the same condition caused by overindulgence will get over it in about twenty-four hours. In some cases, however, the patient may get well faster if nonprescription medications are administered. Both the overindulging human and the food-stealing dog may benefit from a few doses of an appropriate OTC antidiarrheal product.

Conditions that will respond favorably to nonprescription drugs

Many canine medical conditions respond well to nonprescription drugs. An example of this type of condition is flea dermatitis. A veterinarian or a pet shop can supply an owner with a variety of medications that kill fleas in every stage of development. Until recently, only a veterinarian could prescribe oral or topical medications that eliminate fleas by preventing them from reproducing. These and similar drugs are now available on the nonprescription market.

In some cases, prescription-only drugs may have the same action but greater efficacy than OTC drugs recommended for the same condition. For example, an owner with an arthritic dog can try the same OTC drugs that are used for pain in arthritic humans, but at a dose appropriate for dogs. If the dog fails to respond to the nonprescription treatment, the owner can consult a veterinarian for a prescription drug that may help his dog more.

Conditions that require professional veterinary care
All emergency situations require professional care. If your dog is hit by a car and you suspect it may have a serious injury, don't try to treat it with an OTC drug, just as you would not give your child a couple of aspirin if he had a similar injury. Chapters 1 and 2 will help you recognize which conditions are emergencies and which are not.

—

If there is a question that any condition is an
emergency, don't wait.
Consult your veterinarian.

—

Routine medical treatment such as vaccinations and procedures such as fecal examinations can only be done by a veterinarian, for two reasons. Only a veterinarian has the equipment and products that are necessary to carry out the procedures, and the training to know what to do and when to do it. In some areas, owners can buy "shots" for their own dogs, but can owners determine which shots the dog needs and when it is best to give the shots? If owners guess wrong, their dogs may be subject to contracting diseases that professional veterinary care would have prevented. Owners can buy "worm medicine" in almost any pet shop, but if they administer medicine to their dogs without fecal examinations, how do they know if they are giving a medication that will eliminate the dog's internal parasites? How do they know if their dogs have any internal parasites at all? Their dogs may not be helped by the treatment; in fact, their dogs may actually be harmed if they give inappropriate medication.

It is a false economy for an owner to attempt to provide his dog's routine medical care himself. If the dog gets sick, the veterinary bills will be higher than if correct professional care had prevented the illness. Chapter 3 contains details concerning routine veterinary procedures.

Conditions that cannot be cured

Some dog patients, like some human patients, cannot be cured. As do human physicians, veterinarians often recognize conditions that cannot be treated successfully even by the most advanced professional care. Just as in human medicine, there are drugs available to keep the patient comfortable. Only a veterinarian can prescribe narcotics and other restricted painkillers that a critically ill dog may need.

TYPES OF DRUGS AVAILABLE IN THE UNITED STATES

Prescription drugs

The world *prescription* is from the Latin *pre*, meaning "before," and *scriptus*, "to write." The symbol Rx, which signifies "to take," is often used to mean a prescription. Prescription drugs are available only with written or telephone instructions from a medical professional who is licensed to direct the use of these restricted drugs. At this time, only medical doctors (M.D.s, D.O.s), dentists (D.D.S.s), and veterinarians (D.V.M.s, V.M.D.s) are licensed to prescribe drugs in the United States. Osteopaths, chiropractors, and podiatrists are not.

Many prescription drugs are sold under a brand name that is patented by the manufacturer. Some prescription drugs are also available in generic form. When the patent expires, other manufacturers are permitted to produce the drugs under their own brand names or as a generic product. Brand-name drugs and their generic forms are supposed to be identical, but in some cases they are not.

Prescription drugs may be licensed for human or for animal use. Some drugs are licensed with one brand name for humans, a different brand name and a different strength for animals. *Furosemide*, a commonly used diuretic, is an example of this type of drug. Prescriptions for humans are for Lasix, 20-, 40-, or 80-milligram tablets. Prescriptions for dogs are for Lasix or Distal, 12.5- or 50-milligram tablets.

Drugs that are prescription in one strength and are nonprescription in another

A number of drugs that were originally prescription-only have entered the OTC market in a reduced strength or a different form. An example of this is the human drug Tagamet HB 200 (SmithKline Beckman), an OTC tablet that contains 200 milligrams of the drug *cimetidine*. Tagamet as a prescription-only drug is the same drug (cimetidine) available from the same manufacturer in preparations of 200, 300, 400, and 800 milligrams, as well as an oral liquid and an injectable form.

Another example is prescription Motrin, which is *ibuprofen* sold in tablets of 300, 400, 600, or 800 milligrams, and nonprescription Advil, which is the same drug, ibuprofen, sold in 200-milligram tablets.

Several drugs that are routinely prescribed or dispensed by veterinarians are available in nonprescription forms. Hydrocortisone ointment is one example; the prescription drug and the OTC preparations differ mainly in strength and price. It is perfectly acceptable for an owner to ask the prescribing veterinarian if the nonprescription product is adequate to treat the condition, and how the directions need be altered for the use of the OTC medication.

Some nonprescription forms of prescription drugs are available as both a brand name and a generic. Invariably the generic drug is less costly.

Over-the-counter, or nonprescription, drugs

The terms *OTC* and *NPD* (nonprescription drug) mean the same thing: drugs that can be purchased without a prescription. Owners can walk into any drugstore or any pet shop or feed store to buy OTC drugs for themselves or for their animals. Aspirin, Kaopectate, flea powder, some worm medicines, iodine, shampoo—the list is endless and the American public buys them all.

Nonprescription drugs can be anything the manufacturer wants to sell that is not restricted by law. Nonprescription drugs can contain one drug, two drugs, or a combination of several drugs. An OTC drug can be a nationally advertised brand name, Tylenol, for example, or the same drug sold under its generic name, *acetaminophen*.

ORAL MEDICATIONS

Tablets, capsules, liquids, powder—these are only a few of the forms in which drugs can be purchased. Many drugs are available in more than one oral form, which gives dog owners more than one choice of a method of administration. Administering oral medication to a dog is comparable to administering oral medication to a child. The owner or the parent must select the form that is most readily accepted by the dog or by the child. In some cases this will be a tablet hidden in food; in some cases it will be a liquid administered with a medicine dropper, a syringe, or a teaspoon directly into the mouth. In some cases it will be a tablet that is actually pushed down the patient's throat. This technique is often used in dogs but seldom used in children.

TOPICAL MEDICATIONS

Topical preparations are available in ointments, cremes, sprays, powders, and dips. Drugs that are applied to the skin and absorbed by the body to produce a whole-body effect on the patient have recently become available. An example of this type of preparation is the "one spot" systemic flea killers for dogs.

MOST DRUGS ARE SUPPLIED IN METRIC UNITS

The attempt to convert the United States to the metric system of weights and measures met with dismal failure—except in the drug industry. Almost all drugs for oral use are sold only in *milligram* or *milliliter* doses. Familiarity with metric measurements is necessary to use OTC drugs correctly.

———

A *gram* is .035 ounce; the abbreviation is *gm*.

A *milligram* is 1/1,000 of a gram; the abbreviation is *mg*.

A *kilogram* is 1,000 grams, abbreviated *kg*. A kilogram is equivalent to a little less than ½ pound.

A *pound* is about 2.2 kilograms. An *ounce* is equivalent to about 28 grams, or .000035 pounds.

A *liter* is a liquid measure equal to a little less than a quart.

A *milliliter* equals 1/1,000 liter. Thirty milliliters is approximately an ounce.

A *cubic centimeter*, abbreviated *cc*, is a liquid measure that is the same as a milliliter. Oral liquids are often administered by the cc; droppers supplied with many oral preparations are calibrated in ccs.

———

The notable exception to the metric measurement of drugs is the common aspirin tablet. Aspirin has traditionally been supplied in 5-grain tablets. A *grain* equals approximately 60 milligrams; a 5-grain aspirin tablet contains 325 milligrams of the drug. "Baby" aspirin tablets are one fourth of the standard tablet: 1¼ grains, or just over 80 milligrams.

DRUGS AVAILABLE BY THE OUNCE OR POUND

The majority of drugs in this country that are sold by the ounce or pound are intended for topical use. Examples of this type of medication are liquid dips and flea powders. A few oral vitamin-mineral preparations are sold in large quantities and are intended for use in livestock.

THE STATUS OF A DRUG IS SUBJECT TO CHANGE

New drugs are constantly under development, patents on older drugs expire, drugs that were formerly available only under brand names appear as generics. The status of some drugs changes from prescription only to nonprescription. Successful drugs (those with big sales and proven effectiveness) tend to have imitators, both in the prescription and NPD fields. Drugs appear on the market advertised as similar to brand X and "just as good." Often they are; occasionally they are not. Drug manufacturing, distributing, and sales are a multibillion-dollar business. It is up to an owner to be an informed consumer both for human and animal drug products.

LEGAL CONSIDERATIONS WHEN USING OTC DRUGS

All drug labels bear a statement to this affect: *Use only as directed.* This statement is intended to relieve the manufacturer or supplier of legal responsibility if anything goes wrong.

The medical profession has coined the term *extra-label* (or *off-label*) to indicate the use of a drug for any purpose or at any dose other than that indicated on the package or on the package insert. Medical doctors are required to inform patients (and veterinarians are required to inform owners) if they prescribe an extra-label use of a drug. Medical personnel are also required to obtain written consent from the patient or owner for the extra-label use of drugs.

Extra-label (or off-label) use of a drug must meet one or more of these criteria:

- The use of a drug in a species other than the species for which the drug is intended.
- The use of a drug for a condition other than that for which the drug is specifically labeled.
- The use of a drug is a dose other than that which is indicated on the package.

The manufacturer, supplier, or retail sales source is *never* liable for the results of the extra-label use of any drug.

Although *extra-label* is a term commonly applied to prescription drugs, the term can be applied to nonprescription drugs as well. The use of a human drug in other species is always extra-label, since the label carries no instructions for use in a species other than human. If an owner buys a human OTC preparation and uses it for a dog, the manufacturer is never responsible if the results are not as expected.

———

Note: A significant number of human prescription drugs are used and prescribed by veterinarians, especially by small-animal practitioners. The use of human drugs by veterinarians is not considered extra-label if the drugs exist in an identical form, but with a different label, for use by veterinarians for their animal patients.

———

PART I

WHAT CONDITIONS
REQUIRE VETERINARY ATTENTION?

WHICH CONDITIONS
CAN OWNERS TREAT AT HOME?

SIGNS OF PAIN OR DISEASE IN THE DOG

Any change in a dog's normal behavior or appearance is a signal to an observant owner to search for an explanation. *Is the dog in pain? Is the dog sick?* Are the changes in its behavior or appearance caused by a nonmedical condition?

SIGNS OF PAIN

Dogs perceive and react to the sensations we call *pain* in a manner similar to humans. However, since dogs cannot tell you when they're hurting, they must express their discomfort in other ways.

Acute pain

An owner normally has no difficulty recognizing the signs of acute pain. The dog in acute pain may whimper, cry, or bark in distress. A dog may refuse to use an acutely painful limb or may walk with a severe limp. A dog with acute abdominal pain may remain lying down and vigorously resist attempts to force it to rise. A dog in acute pain is likely to demonstrate hysterical or defensive biting directed toward anyone—including its owner—who attempts to handle the painful portion of its body.

Puppies are more likely to cry out in acute pain than are mature dogs. This may be because the instinct to seek maternal attention is still strongly present in puppies. Just as do human children, puppies often cry vigorously when they suffer a minor painful occurrence, only to forget about it and resume normal activity within ten minutes. Adult dogs experiencing acute pain often are silent unless forced to move the painful area.

Breed differences in pain response are less significant than individual differences. Dogs of every breed that are well socialized are more likely to express pain by whining or crying than are dogs that have had little human contact. Small and toy breeds often whine or cry with less provocation. Fear is a likely cause of this tendency.

The first aim of treatment should be identifying and eliminating the cause of the pain. X rays, ultrasound, MRI, and CAT scans are modern methods to determine the reasons behind the pain in both humans and dogs.

Chronic pain

It is much more difficult for an owner to recognize the signs of chronic pain than to recognize the signs of acute pain. Because chronic pain may come on slowly, the dog's behavior may not obviously reveal the pain's presence.

Chronic pain may appear to be present in both hind limbs such as hip dysplasia or spinal cord disease. Chronic pain that consistently occurs in a single limb, especially if swelling is present, is a danger sign of a serious condition such as bone cancer.

Often, chronic pain is related to aging. An owner may notice that it is more difficult for the dog to stand from a sitting or lying position, especially after sleeping. When the dog struggles to its feet, its gait may be stiff and abnormal. At first the dog's gait may improve after mild exercise. Eventually the dog is reluctant or unable to exercise at all. A dog suffering from chronic pain may gain weight because of its relative inactivity. If the dog's inactivity is severe or prolonged, wasting of its muscles, especially in the hindquarters, may become apparent. A dog in chronic pain may whine or groan when it changes position in its sleep.

Since a dog cannot describe the location of its pain, its response to medication can contribute to a diagnosis. El-

derly dogs that improve when given anti-inflammatory
drugs are likely to be suffering from chronic arthritis.
Arthritic joint changes are the most common cause of
chronic pain in the aging dog. Many breeds are predisposed
toward joint abnormalities that lead to arthritis, dogs with
hip dysplasia and resulting arthritic hip joints being the
classic example.

The treatment of chronic pain in dogs is similar to the
treatment of chronic pain in humans. Prescription steroid
medications such as cortisone and related drugs often are
used, though these drugs may have side effects if used for
long periods of time. Nonsteroidal anti-inflammatory drugs
(NSAIDs) such as aspirin, nutritional supplements, and related medications are useful for the treatment of chronic
arthritic pain in dogs and in humans. Many of these drugs
are available in nonprescription forms.

CONTROLLING PAIN IN THE DOG

The selection of a medication to reduce pain is dependent on
the species of the patient, the desired interval of administration, the side effects of the medication, and to a limited
extent, the cost and availability of the drugs.

NONSTEROIDAL ANTI-INFLAMMATORY DRUGS

Among the most frequently purchased nonprescription medications are NSAIDs, which control pain and reduce inflammation and fever in the human patient. People are willing to
buy and use a great number of products if they think that the
medications will make them feel better.

Owners want their dogs to feel better, too. Human over-
the-counter drugs for pain, inflammation, and fever are in
wide use for dogs for postsurgical pain, injuries, and joint
conditions such as hip dysplasia and osteoarthritis. In many
instances, the use of human NSAIDs for dogs is entirely ap-

propriate and beneficial *only* when the drug is given in doses and at intervals that are correct for dogs.

The action of NSAIDs

Nonsteroidal anti-inflammatory drugs act to inhibit one type of a group of chemical substances called *prostaglandins* that are released in inflammatory processes in the body. By this action, NSAIDs prevent or reduce tissue swelling and pain.

Unfortunately, NSAID drugs also inhibit the action of another type of prostaglandin that protects internal organs such as the liver, the stomach, and the kidneys, and promotes the normal clotting of blood. It is essential to administer enough of a NSAID to relieve inflammation and pain but not enough to cause harm to the patient.

How to Use NSAIDs

- Weigh the patient and calculate the dose of each NSAID drug.
- Never exceed the dose or give the drug more frequently than indicated.
- Use the smallest dose and the longest interval that will produce the desired effect.
- Always administer NSAID drugs with food.

New NSAIDs are under development that have the same anti-inflammatory action as the older ones but that do not inhibit the prostaglandins that protect internal organs. These drugs are far safer than the drugs currently available. The drugs are available by prescription only for humans and dogs. It may be many years before the new NSAIDs reach the nonprescription market.

NSAIDs in combination with other drugs

A large number of human nonprescription drugs that contain NSAIDs also contain other drugs such as antihistamines and cough remedies. These compounds are formulated to treat several symptoms of human illness at the same time. Many of the additional drugs in these compounds have no use in treating dogs' medical conditions. Some of the ingredients in these compounds may be harmful to dogs or may be present in doses that will harm dogs. The correct dose of each of the drugs in a compound may be entirely different for a dog than for a human.

———

Use Only Preparations that Contain a Single Nonsteroidal Anti-inflammatory Drug.

———

The exceptions to this rule are the aspirin preparations that also contain buffering agents. Chemically, aspirin is an acid. A dog's stomach contents are normally more acid than a human's stomach contents. The buffering agents intended to prevent human stomach irritation are neither necessary nor harmful to the dog.

Generic or brand names?

Almost every nonprescription nonsteroidal anti-inflammatory drug is available in both brand names and as generic preparations. Some of the brand names as well as some of the generics have certain advantages. Some are available in children's-size doses that are useful for small dogs. "Canine" aspirin preparations, available in pet shops and pet supply catalogs, are often liver-flavored chewable tablets.

Generic drugs are often identical to brand names, at a significantly lower cost. Drugs do not appreciate the amenities that are attractive to children, such as the flavoring and coloring present in some brand names. It is certainly less costly to hide a generic human aspirin tablet in a piece of cheese than it is to purchase liver-flavored "dog aspirin." For long-term use in humans and animals, generic preparations are the obvious economic choice.

Which of the currently available non-presription anti-inflammatory drugs are best for medicating dogs?

First choice: *Aspirin*. Aspirin has properties that effectively reduce inflammation, pain, and fever. Aspirin has been proven to be safe for long-term use in most species. Aspirin is available in several tablet sizes as well as in liquid preparations. Aspirin, especially in generic form, is inexpensive.

As with every drug, there are a few contraindications for the use of aspirin. A few dogs tolerate aspirin poorly. Gastric irritation, which is common in humans, occurs rarely in the dog. A dog that vomits after being given aspirin should be given another drug or should not be given aspirin on an empty stomach. Aspirin should not be used for pregnant dogs since there is a chance that the drug may harm unborn puppies.

To maintain its effect, aspirin must be administered at eight- to twelve-hour intervals in the dog.

Second Choice: *Ibuprofin*. The anti-inflammatory and pain-relieving properties of ibuprofen are similar to those of aspirin. Ibuprofen has not been proven as safe as aspirin for long-term continuous use in humans or dogs. The advantage to using ibuprofen for pain and inflammation is that *the drug need not—in fact, **must not**—be administered to a dog more often than once every twenty-four to forty-eight hours*. The long duration of its effect may make this drug convenient for some owners to use.

Third choice: *Acetaminophen*. Acetaminophen is a useful drug for pain only. It is not a true nonsteroidal anti-inflammatory drug, as it has little if any anti-inflammatory effect.

Effective for human headache pain, acetaminophen is not ordinarily recommended for conditions in which the anti-inflammatory function of the drug is important. Acetaminophen is not as effective as either aspirin or ibuprofen in treating osteoarthritis or similar conditions of dogs.

Last Choice: *Naproxen.* Naproxin is a relatively new NSAID on the nonprescription market. This drug has a lower margin of safety in the dog than either aspirin or ibuprofen. It is not difficult to administer an overdose of naproxin to a dog. An overdose may have adverse effect on dogs' kidney and liver function. As with ibuprofen, *naproxin **must not** be administered to a dog more often than once in twenty-four hours.*

Naproxin probably has more use in treating humans and other species than dogs. The drug is often used in horses for treating lameness and muscle spasms.

—

WARNING!
Overdose of NSAIDs can cause irreversible damage to kidneys and other organs.
NEVER EXCEED THE RECOMMENDED DOSE.

—

SIGNS OF DISEASE

In the medical dictionary, *disease* is defined as "any departure from a state of health." Disease can be minor or life threatening, acute or chronic. A disease can involve only one organ or the entire body. Any abnormal condition from fleabite allergy to metastatic cancer can be called a disease.

Infectious diseases
Conditions caused by agents such as bacteria, viruses, protozoa, and parasites are ***infectious diseases***. Infectious diseases can be ***contagious*** if the agent is transmissible to other animals. For example, an outer-ear infection caused by bacteria is not contagious to an uninfected dog; an outer-ear infection caused by ear mites is contagious since the mites are readily spread from one animal to another.

Some infectious diseases are contagious only to closely related species of animals. For example, the virus of canine distemper affects only dogs and doglike animals. Other in-

fectious diseases are contagious to a wide variety of animals.
The rabies virus will infect almost every warm-blooded
species.

An important characteristic of many infectious and contagious diseases is that animals can be rendered less susceptible to the condition by the administration of *vaccines*.

Infectious disease should be suspected if a susceptible
animal has a history of exposure to the infectious agent. For
example, a sick puppy should be suspected of having canine
distemper if it came from an animal shelter where the distemper virus is common. If the puppy has been rendered less
susceptible by being vaccinated, there is a much greater
chance that it is suffering from another condition.

Nonprescription NSAIDs for Dogs

DRUG	SOME BRAND NAMES	HOW SUPPLIED
Acetaminophen	TYLENOL Regular Strength	325-mg tablets
	TYLENOL Extra Strength	500-mg tablets
	GENERIC PREPARATIONS	325-mg & 500-mg tablets

Dose: 8 mg per pound of body weight, every 8 hours. A 25-lb dog
would receive 200 mg every 8 hours. This is about ¾ of a single
human tablet.

Comments: For pain only. Little or no anti-inflammatory action.
Other NSAIDs are more effective for arthritic conditions in dogs.

Aspirin (acetylsalicylic acid)	ASCRIPTIN	325-mg buffered tablets
	GENUINE BAYER ASPIRIN	325-mg tablets
	EXTRA STRENGTH BAYER	500-mg tablet & caplets

Nonprescription NSAIDs for Dogs (*continued*)

DRUG	SOME BRAND NAMES	HOW SUPPLIED
	BAYER CHILDREN'S CHEWABLE	81-mg tablets
	ST. JOSEPH'S ADULT CHEWABLE TABLETS	81-mg tablets
	CANINE ASPIRIN PREPARATIONS (chewables)	120-mg & 600-mg tablets
	GENERIC PREPARATIONS	325-mg & 81-mg tablets

Dose: 5 to 10 mg per pound of body weight. A 25-lb dog would need 125 to 250 mg every 8 hours, or about ¾ of a human adult-sized tablet; a 50-lb dog would need one or 1½ tablets every 8 hours. It is easier to use the low-dose tablets for small dogs.

Comments: Aspirin is the best and safest choice of currently available nonprescription NSAIDs for dogs.

Ibuprofen	ADVIL	200-mg tablets & caplets
	CHILDREN'S MOTRIN	50-mg chewable tablets
	MOTRIN IB PAIN RELIEVER	220-mg tablets & caplets
	NUPRIN	200-mg tablets & caplets
	GENERIC PREPARATIONS	200-mg tablets & caplets

Dose: 2.5 to 5 mg per pound of body weight. Given only every 24 to 48 hours. A 25-lb dog would receive 75 to 150 mg or approximately ½ an adult tablet; a 50-lb dog would receive one human adult-sized tablet.

Nonprescription NSAIDs for Dogs (*continued*)

DRUG	SOME BRAND NAMES	HOW SUPPLIED

Comments: Long interval between doses. Very toxic to cats.

Naproxen	ALEVE	220-mg tablets or caplets

Dose: ½ to 1 mg per pound of body weight every 24 hours. A 25-lb dog should be given no more than 25 mg, which is approximately ¼ of a human tablet. A 50-lb dog should receive only ½ of a human tablet every 24 hours.

Comments: The safety of naproxen has not been established for use in dogs.

Noninfectious diseases

Abnormalities that occur when something goes wrong with an animal's body are *noninfectious* diseases. In some cases, the causes of noninfectious diseases are not entirely known. Cancers may be caused by genetic abnormalities, exposure to carcinogens, as well as other factors. Kidney failure is often caused by ingestion of toxic materials such as antifreeze. Noninfectious diseases should be suspected if the patient has access to disease-producing substances.

However, noninfectious diseases may occur even when exposure to harmful agents has not been observed. The vomiting dog might have found and eaten a dead bird in its own backyard. The sick puppy may have contacted a virus while on its daily walk.

Degenerative diseases

Conditions that result from normal or abnormal degeneration of a portion of the body are *degenerative diseases.* Arthritis is a degenerative disease that often occurs in the joints of old dogs and old people. Abnormal bone formation in the spine is a degenerative disease that can result in locomotor difficulties in middle-aged or old dogs. Senile cataracts form when the lenses of aging eyes undergo degenerative changes.

A disease may have several names

Many diseases are given the same or similar names, regardless of the cause of the condition. For example, *hepatitis* is an inflammation of the liver. Hepatitis caused by a virus is correctly termed *viral hepatitis*. If a toxin causes the condition, it is termed *toxic hepatitis*.

SIGNS OF DISEASE IN THE DOG

A *sign* is an indication of a disease process in an animal's body. The type of sign depends on the part of the animal's body that is affected. Early signs of many different diseases are identical.

• **Listlessness, decreased activity, and failure to eat** are the earliest signs of disease in dogs and puppies. These signs are easily recognized. If a dog remains listless and refuses to eat for more than twenty-four hours, a serious condition may be developing and a veterinarian should be consulted.

• **Fever** is an early sign in many infectious and some noninfectious diseases. The normal temperature of a dog is variable: the normal temperature of a small dog is higher than that of a large one; the normal temperature of a puppy is higher than that of an adult; the normal temperature of an excited dog is higher than that of a calm dog.

As a general rule, the normal temperature of a dog is **99.5** degrees F to **102.5** degrees F. Any temperature over 102 degrees F in an adult dog and 103 degrees F in a puppy should be regarded as abnormal. A dog's body temperature is determined exactly as is the body temperature of a child: by use of a rectal thermometer. Any thermometer suitable for taking the temperature of an infant is suitable for taking the temperature of a dog or puppy.

• **Vomiting** is an indication that the animal is suffering from gastritis, which is an inflammation of the lining of the stomach. *Productive vomiting* occurs when the vomitus contains recognizable material. Productive vomiting often reveals the cause of the dog's gastritis: worms, bones, foreign material, and other indigestible articles. Fortunately for the dog, vomiting after eating irritating substances is often a reflex action. If the dog appears to be normal after vomiting, it probably does not need further treatment.

Unproductive vomiting occurs when an animal retches or attempts to vomit and nothing is emitted except stomach acids or greenish-yellow fluid. Unproductive vomiting is a much more serious sign in the dog than is productive vomiting. An intestine blocked by a foreign body or a disease process in other parts of the dog's body may cause the dog to vomit unproductively. If the condition persists for more than six hours, the dog should be seen by a veterinarian.

• **Diarrhea** is defined as stool consistency of anything from unformed to completely watery. Unformed stools are a common result of overeating, internal parasites, and eating spoiled food. A dog with diarrhea that is frisky and willing to eat is probably not very sick. A dog that has diarrhea and is also listless and vomiting should have veterinary attention. An important danger sign in the dog is watery diarrhea that contains dark, foul-smelling blood—call your veterinarian right away.

• **Abnormal bleeding** is usually a serious sign of disease. Blood in a dog's urine, stool, or vomitus is an indication that a prompt visit to a veterinarian is required.

Puppies may have very mild bleeding from the gums when they lose their first teeth. Dogs may have very slightly blood-streaked stools as a result of passing bone fragments. A veterinarian should be consulted if any significant amount of blood is lost or if bleeding is observed more than once.

• **Abnormal discharges** from the eyes, nose, penis, or vulva are signs that the organs involved are not normal. Nasal and ocular discharges are common in upper respiratory disease and in pneumonia, and are a secondary condition in canine distemper. Of particular significance is vaginal discharge in middle-aged or older unspayed females. Especially if other signs of illness accompany the discharge, a vaginal discharge can be an indication of life-threatening uterine infections. In cases such as this, a veterinarian should be consulted promptly.

• **Coughing** indicates a problem of the throat or the lungs. A suddenly appearing, continuous harsh cough can indicate viral *tracheobronchitis* (kennel cough), a condition in which a disease has caused inflammation of the windpipe and airways.

A harsh cough that becomes more frequent over time may indicate fluid buildup in the patient's lungs, caused by congestive heart failure or heartworm disease.

• **Exercise intolerance and difficulty breathing** occur in a dog that appears to be normal when at rest but quickly becomes tired or collapses when forced to exercise. As with a chronic cough, these conditions often are the result of heart disease and require veterinary attention.

• **Abnormally increased water consumption, with or without increased frequency or volume of urination** may indicate kidney disease or other conditions such as diabetes that require professional veterinary attention.

• **Straining to urinate or the inability to urinate** is an indication of a serious abnormality of the urinary tract. A veterinarian must see any dog that is unable to urinate freely within a few hours.

• **Seizures or loss of consciousness** in a dog are dramatic indications that the dog's nervous system is malfunctioning. Seizures may originate in the brain. Seizures may also be caused by toxic substances that were eaten or metabolic disturbances in other parts of the body. A veterinarian must see any dog that has frequent or persistent seizures.

• **Unexplained lumps, bumps, or swellings** on a dog need professional diagnosis, especially those that increase in size and/or produce signs such as lameness. Many such masses have no impact on the health of the dog, but it is wise to be sure that these masses are not tumors.

Any dog with a gradually enlarging abdomen that cannot be accredited to normal causes such as pregnancy or obesity may be suffering from one of several diseases. *Metritis* (pus in the uterus), *ascites* (fluid in the abdominal cavity), and *abdominal tumors* are a few of the conditions that require prompt treatment if the patient is to survive.

• **Scratching, loss of hair, or lesions of the skin** may indicate disease conditions that are caused by parasites or allergies. Correct treatment of skin lesions requires the identification and control of the causative agents that may require veterinary attention.

2

EMERGENCIES:
RUSH TO A VETERINARIAN RIGHT NOW!

A *TRUE EMERGENCY* is a situation in which the patient will die unless it receives immediate medical attention. A dog that was struck by a car and is semiconscious and bleeding internally is an example of a true emergency.

A *HUMANE EMERGENCY* occurs when the victim probably will not die, but will suffer needless pain and distress unless it is treated promptly. In these instances, delay in treatment also will allow infection and tissue damage to make treatment more difficult. A dog with a broken leg is an example of a humane emergency.

An *APPARENT EMERGENCY* is one in which the victim seems to be badly hurt, but actually is not. A puppy that yelps loudly when stepped on, but acts perfectly normal within ten minutes, is not an emergency.

When there is a doubt, every case should be considered a true emergency

---

SERIOUS INJURIES

Many accidents or incidents can result in an injury to a dog: a dog is hit by a car, a dog falls off the porch, or a dog is attacked by another dog. Often, dogs that are allowed to run loose suffer injuries unobserved and limp home—if they are able to walk at all.

A dog can be assumed to have suffered an injury if it has any of these signs:

• A dog is suddenly **lame,** cannot use one limb, or cannot walk at all. An injured limb may be dangling or misshapen. A dog with pelvic or spinal damage may be unable to get to its feet.

A dog with a broken leg or spinal injuries must be transported without causing additional trauma. Because injured dogs are likely to bite from pain and fear, it may be necessary to muzzle an injured dog in order to help it. After muzzling, carry the dog on an improvised stretcher made from a blanket or a coat.

• The dog has **profuse bleeding** from a natural body opening or from the site of an injury. If possible, significant bleeding should be stopped by applying compression to the area. If a limb is bleeding, the entire limb must be wrapped tightly with clean bandages or cloths. The wrapping must include the paw below the injury.

• The dog is **unconscious** or acts dazed. These conditions indicate serious head injury or early signs of life-threatening shock.

• The dog has signs of **shock.** The medical definition of *shock* is "a condition of acute circulatory failure." Circulatory failure is anything that disrupts the body's ability to maintain normal blood pressure, such as internal or external bleeding.

Early signs of shock include weakness; feeble, rapid pulse; slow, shallow breathing; restlessness; and anxiety. Pale skin in humans that are in shock is a sign that is not easy to see in the dog, but pale gums can be detected in all but black-lipped dogs. Dogs in shock also have cold extremities such as paws and ears.

Shock is a true medical emergency. Unconsciousness and death are the eventual result if normal blood pressure is not restored. Dogs suspected of being in shock must be kept warm, kept still, and transported to a veterinary hospital or veterinary emergency clinic with all speed possible.

SUDDEN DIFFICULTY IN BREATHING

Any animal that cannot get enough oxygen into its body is at serious risk of death. If it cannot get any oxygen into its lungs, it will die within minutes.

Most conditions of *dyspnea* (difficult breathing) come on gradually. Fluid buildup in the lungs is one cause of gradually increasing breathing difficulty. A dog that pants excessively, that has a chronic cough, or that becomes tired with only a little exercise in experiencing gradual increase of dyspnea. Such a dog's medical problem must be diagnosed and treated by a veterinarian long before it has reached a critical stage.

Dyspnea that comes on suddenly is not common. Some causes of this type of condition are

- a foreign body lodged in the trachea
- a torn, collapsed, or paralyzed trachea
- a penetrating wound to the chest wall that allows air to enter the thorax and cause the lungs to collapse
- a diaphragmatic hernia in which the dog has sustained trauma to the abdomen that results in the internal organs being displaced into the chest

Cases such as these present an immediate threat to the patient's life. Any time a dog seems to be struggling or gasping for breath, it must be rushed to a veterinary facility. It will be a lucky dog that receives treatment quickly enough to prevent asphyxiation.

INABILITY TO GIVE BIRTH NORMALLY

Dystocia is the medical term for difficult birth. When dystocia occurs, the puppies may be lost, the mother dogs may be lost, all of them may be lost. Medical help is essential whenever a female is unable to whelp normally.

Fortunately, most dogs whelp without difficulty. Females in active labor normally produce a puppy every few minutes. If a dog labors for more than two hours before delivering the first puppy or more than an hour between puppies, the dog and the puppies that have already been born should be rushed to a veterinarian or to an emergency clinic.

Dystocia is a true emergency. In extreme cases, the mother dogs may need a cesarean section to save her life and that of her litter.

3

ROUTINE CARE: *MAKE A VETERINARY APPOINTMENT THIS WEEK*

Regular professional medical care is just as important for dogs as it is for humans. Puppies need vaccinations and parasite control to get them off to a good start in life. Mature dogs ordinarily require only a few professional services to maintain health while geriatric dogs may need additional tests and procedures to prolong their healthy years. The dog that receives basic medical attention is likely to live to old age free of the ravages of preventable disease.

ROUTINE HEALTH CARE FOR PUPPIES AND YOUNG DOGS

The principles of vaccination

An animal is resistant or immune to a disease only when its bloodstream contains *antibodies* against the organism that causes the disease. An animal's body produces antibodies in response to the presence of *antigens,* such as a disease-causing viruses and bacteria. If an animal recovers from a disease, its bloodstream usually contains antibodies that will prevent the animal from catching the disease again.

The purpose of vaccination is to cause an animal to become immune to a disease without it being infected with the actual disease-causing organisms. A vaccine is composed of viruses or bacteria that have been killed or weakened by heat or chemicals. These organisms that have been weakened or killed act as antigens. The body produces antibodies just as if the killed or weakened viruses or bacteria were capable of causing disease. Most vaccines for dogs contain antigens against more than one disease. Some vaccines produce immunity against as many as five diseases with a single injection.

What is "temporary" immunity?

Puppies obtain temporary immunity against disease from the mother dog's *colostrum.* Colostrum is the milk produced by every mammal for the first twelve to twenty-four hours immediately after she has given birth. Colostrum is different from ordinary milk in that it contains the antibodies that are present in the mother's blood. When newborn puppies nurse, they absorb these antibodies into their own bloodstream.

Unlike in humans, the structure of the dog's placenta allows very little passage of the mother's antibodies to the puppies while they are still in the uterus. Therefore, it is important that newborn pups consume their mother's antibody-rich colostrum during the first few hours of their lives. While human infants are born with temporary immunity to the diseases to which their mothers are resistant, puppies must get their immunity from colostrum.

Why do puppies need all those shots?

Colostrum-derived immunity is only temporary. By the time puppies are six to ten weeks of age, their temporary immunity to diseases has decreased or disappeared. However, while the temporary immunity is still active, the antibodies in puppies' blood will destroy not only disease-causing bacteria and viruses, but the immunity-producing antigens in vaccines as well. To become immune to disease, puppies must receive vaccines when their bodies are able to respond to them.

Temporary immunity does not disappear from every puppy's body at the same time. Only a blood test can determine when a puppy's temporary immunity has decreased enough to allow its body to respond to the antigens in a vaccine. It is less expensive and more convenient to administer repeated vaccines to puppies than to have each puppy's blood tested to determine the optimum time to vaccinate it. Therefore, a puppy is given vaccines at two- to four-week intervals until it is at least twelve weeks old, to be sure that it has received a vaccine at the optimum time for its body to produce immunity to disease.

Combination vaccines

At least seven contagious diseases threaten dogs in the United States. Distemper, adenovirus, parainfluenza, parvovirus, leptospirosis, bordetella, and bronchiseptica (kennel cough) are threats to the health of the canine population. Other diseases such as Lyme disease may be present in some parts of the country.

Most vaccines are formulated to provide immunity to at least two and as many as five diseases with one injection. Knowledge of the history and condition of the individual puppy and the prevalence of each disease in the geographic area enables a practicing veterinarian to set up an appropriate vaccination schedule for each animal.

Rabies vaccination

Rabies kills. Rabies kills wildlife, domestic animals, pets, and humans. It is, however, a disease that is almost entirely preventable by vaccination.

Puppies should receive their first rabies vaccination at three months of age. A dog that was vaccinated as a puppy should receive a booster rabies vaccine when it is a year old, then a booster at designated intervals throughout its life. In many states, only veterinarians can legally administer rabies vaccine.

Internal parasites

Except for contagious disease, internal parasites are the greatest threat to the health of puppies. Almost every puppy will become infected with a variety of "worms" while still in the uterus and during the first weeks of life. If the condition is left untreated, a puppy's health and often its life are threatened.

Internal parasites are detected by finding microscopic parasite eggs in the puppy's or dog's stool. At each visit to a veterinarian, a stool sample should be presented for examination under the microscope. After the puppy has been treated for internal parasites, repeated examinations of its stool will show whether all the parasites have been eliminated.

Heartworm prevention

Heartworm disease has become common in almost every area of the United States. The parasite is spread from diseased dogs to healthy dogs by the bite of an affected mosquito.

This killer disease is prevented by destroying the immature forms of the parasites in the dog's body before the parasites can enter the heart and become mature worms. This is accomplished by giving a monthly dose of a preventive drug that is available only from veterinarians.

Every puppy or dog that is more than four months of age must have its blood tested for the presence of heartworms before the preventive medication is administered. A dog that is infected with heartworms must be cleared of the parasite before it can be placed on a preventive program.

Spay and neuter surgery

Every dog that is not intended to reproduce should be surgically altered. The dog's health will be better and its behavior more socially acceptable than those that are not spayed or neutered.

Recent studies have shown that dogs can be spayed and neutered as young as eight weeks of age without any adverse affects. The surgery should be scheduled at the convenience of the owner and the veterinarian.

HEALTH MAINTENANCE FOR THE MATURE DOG

When a dog has been immunized against contagious diseases and is free of internal parasites, its routine health maintenance consists of a few simple procedures.

Routine physical examination
A dog's annual checkup by a veterinarian is as important as is a human's annual checkup by a physician. During the examination, the doctor will examine the patient's eyes and ears, listen to the patient's heart, check for unusual lumps or discharges, and answer questions pertaining to the patient's health, recommending additional tests if necessary.

Routine booster vaccinations
Booster vaccinations against the major contagious diseases are recommended for some conditions. The administration of these vaccines helps to keep the patient's immunity at its highest level.

Routine dental work
A routine physical examination for a dog includes an inspection of the dog's mouth and teeth. Neglected tartar buildup, gum disease, and broken teeth can affect the dog's overall health, not just the condition of its mouth. Since almost all dental work on dogs is done under general anesthesia, dental care, if needed, can be scheduled for another appointment.

Routine examination for parasites, including heartworm
A fecal examination for the presence of internal parasites and a blood test for heartworm larvae are included in a rou-

tine physical examination. If either of the tests is positive, corrective action can be taken.

HEALTH CARE FOR THE GERIATRIC DOG

Geriatric dogs may require annual physical check-ups. The larger the breed, the sooner a dog becomes geriatric. A Great Dane may be in its senior years when it is only six or seven years of age; a Pekingese may not be physically old until it is twelve or even older.

The purpose of extra veterinary attention for the older dog is to detect physical problems while they are in the early stages. Most medical conditions of aging are more easily and more successfully handled if treatment is begun before the problems become severe.

Depending on the dog's history, a veterinarian may recommend several laboratory tests to determine the health status of the geriatric dog.

- *Urinalysis:* Diminished kidney function is one of the major medical conditions of old age. An analysis of the dog's urine will detect kidney disease in the early stages.
- *Hematology:* A complete blood count, including a determination of blood enzymes, can disclose abnormal organ function before the patient has signs of illness.
- *Radiology:* If the geriatric dog has unexplained signs of cardiovascular disease, abdominal enlargement, or locomotor difficulty, X rays may be indicated.
- *Electrocardiogram, ultrasound examination, or other specialized tests:* These can be done in some veterinary practices and at most referral clinics. Tests of this sort are needed only for dogs with problems that cannot be diagnosed by other means.

4

HOW TO SELECT A DRUG AND CALCULATE
THE CORRECT DOSE

—

Every use of human medications in the dog is extra-label.
Owners use these drugs for their dogs at their own risk.

—

MEDICATIONS FORMULATED FOR DOGS

Calculating the correct dose of drugs formulated for use in
the dog is simplicity itself: the directions are printed on the
package. Since the metric system of weights and measures
has not been adopted in the United States, the directions for
nonprescription drugs for animal use are all given in *avoir-
dupois* measures. The label will read: one tablet for so many
pounds of body weight of the patient, or so many drops for
every *pound* of body weight of the patient. Drugs sold in
countries that use the metric system will be labeled so many
milligrams for each *kilogram* of body weight.

It is important to read the entire label when using any
medication. If there are restrictions on the use of the medication, it is important to obey them. For example, a medication with a label that reads *for dogs over three months of age*
should not be used on dogs under three months. It is proba-
ble that the manufacturer has determined that the drug may
not be safe in younger puppies.

Some preparations that are sold in pet shops are labeled

as to their use but not as to their ingredients. An example of products of this type is "ear wash" or "ear cleansers" sold for dogs. It is likely that products that do not list an active ingredient do not actually contain an active ingredient. Let the buyer beware!

MEDICATIONS FORMULATED FOR HUMANS

The use of human nonprescription drugs in the dog is an entirely different matter. The labels on nonprescription drugs intended for human adults give appropriate doses of the drug for an average-sized adult. The built-in margin of safety of nonprescription drugs is such that an "adult" dose will be suitable for a human from 100 to more than 200 pounds.

The dose of a human medication for a dog may be very different from the dose for a human. With some drugs, a human adult dose is also a dose safe for an adult dog. With most drugs, however, the human adult dose is too large for all except the giant breeds. And with only a few drugs, a dog requires more medication for each pound of body weight than does a human.

Selecting the form of a human oral medication for a dog
Tablets, caplets (elongated tablets), hard *gelatin capsules,* and *gelcaps* or *soft-gels* (soft capsules) are some of the solid forms in which drugs are manufactured. A few drugs are sold as *powders. Liquid* drugs may be given by the tea-spoonful, the tablespoonful, or the dropperful. Human drugs, especially those intended for children, often include a flavoring agent, such as peppermint or various fruit flavors, to make the drugs more attractive to the human patient.

Many human nonprescription drugs are supplied in several forms. The best form to choose is whichever will simplify administration of the medication to a dog.

• *Tablets* are the most familiar forms of drugs. Tablets are discs of medication containing the drug mixed with an inert binder to keep the tablets in shape. Tablets come in many sizes, shapes, and colors; they are often marked with a code number or a manufacturer's symbol.

Tablets may be coated or uncoated. Coated tablets have an outer layer of a material (often colored) that make them easier to swallow and that is intended to resist the action of human stomach acids. These tablets are designed to dissolve in the human intestines, not the stomach. Coated tablets are never scored, as the inner contents are exposed if they are broken, defeating the intended action of the coating.

Uncoated tablets are often scored with a line on one side. This line is intended to make the tablets easy to break in half for the administration of only half the dose. You will find that only the larger tablets snap in half properly. Small tablets are often difficult to break, but drugstores sell several types of "pill splitters" that will make the job easier. These are little devices that contain a blade that is pressed through the tablet at the score line. If you do not have a pill splitter, you can achieve the same effect with a knife. Place the tablet, scored side up, on a clean piece of paper. Put a sharp knife on the score line and press down with your thumb. The tablet should pop in half. Be careful to prevent the halves of the tablet from flying off into space.

• *Caplets* are the drug industry's solution to the problem of easily tampered-with capsules. Caplets are hard, often coated, elongated tablets. They are actually tablets in capsule shape.

Drugs are supplied in caplet form instead of in tablets when a tablet containing the same amount of medication would be too large for humans to swallow comfortably. Caplets are designed to go down lengthwise through the esophagus.

Uncoated caplets are often scored to make it easy to di-

vide them in half. Since they are larger and elongated, they
break more easily than do round tablets.

• *Capsules* are little containers made of gelatin. Capsules
that contain powdered medication are rigid gelatin and are
made in two pieces; capsules that contain liquids are soft
and made in one piece. The soft capsules are often called
gelcaps or *soft-gels.*

Capsules and soft-gels are intended to be swallowed unbroken, and their coverings are easily dissolved and punc-
tured. Administration of medication in these forms is
therefore difficult unless the drug can be hidden in a piece of
food that the dog will gulp right down.

Some years ago, a criminal purchased several bottles of a
pain medication that was then supplied in hard gelatin capsules. He or she pulled the two halves of some of the capsules apart, filled them with a poisonous substance, then put
the halves back together. The killer then put the capsules
back into the original bottles and returned the bottles to the
store shelves. Some people who purchased these poisoned
capsules died from unknowingly taking the poison.

Since that time, only a few nonprescription drugs are fur-
nished in capsule form, and the two halves of these nonprescription capsules are joined so that the capsules cannot be
opened and then reclosed. In addition, a federal law requires
that all over-the-counter nonprescription medications be
sealed in their containers with a "safety seal" that is broken
when the container is opened. Even with all these precautions, be sure you inspect any medication and the container
in which it is sold before you take any drug or give it to your
dog. If the container appears to have been tampered with, return it to your druggist.

• *Granules (or powders)* for human use are designed to be
mixed with liquids before they are consumed. Obviously, a
dog is not going to drink a glass of orange juice even if it

does not contain medication. If you give your dog granules or powder, you will have to mix it into some food item that the dog will readily eat.

• *Drops* or dropperfuls of medication can be squirted onto the dog's tongue. If the medication is not flavored, it can be applied to the dog's regular food.

• *Liquids* intended to be given by the teaspoonful, table-spoonful, or syringeful—especially those that are peppermint or fruit flavored—are the most difficult of all medications to administer. Most dogs will resist taking these drugs, and will try to spit them out. It is impossible to administer an accurate amount of these medications; much of each dose will be on the dog's coat and the owner's clothing.

Brand name or generic?

Many human drugs are available both in a patented brand name and a generic form. In some cases, the brand name will contain extra ingredients such as color or flavoring. In the majority of cases, the brand name and the equivalent generic product will be identical except for price. When items are identical, it makes good sense to choose the least expensive for use in humans as well as in dogs.

As an example, Ascriptin lists as the ingredients in each tablet: "aspirin (325 mg) buffered with alumina-magnesia and calcium carbonate." Most generic buffered aspirin lists as its ingredients in each tablet: "aspirin (325 mg)" buffered with calcium carbonate and one or more other buffering agents. Which is superior, the brand name or the generic? Probably both drugs are equal in efficacy and safety.

Some drugs have special features. For example, Genuine Bayer Aspirin tablets and caplets are coated with an inactive ingredient designed to make swallowing easier. The comparable generic form of aspirin would be labeled: "Coated Aspirin." Special features are rarely useful in a medication that is administered to dogs, since tablets are most often given to dogs in pieces of food.

Most human nonprescription drugs intended for oral use will have the active ingredients listed in milligrams for each unit of the product. Solid products will list the active ingredients contained in each tablet or capsule; liquid products will list the active ingredients contained in each teaspoonful, each dropperful, or each drop. For example, Ascriptin lists as its active ingredient "aspirin, 325 mg." This means that every tablet of the product contains 325 milligrams of aspirin. Children's Motrin Oral Suspension lists "ibuprofen, 100 mg" as its active ingredient. Each teaspoonful (5 ml) of the product contains 100 milligrams of ibuprofen.

—

Avoid Human Drugs Containing Several Ingredients

Many brand-name nonprescription medications are a combination of several active ingredients. An example of these is the patented "cold and cough remedies" that contain a drug for pain, a decongestant, and an antihistamine. Since the dose for each of the ingredients may be entirely different for dogs than for humans, formulas that contain several active ingredients are inappropriate for use in the dog.

—

CALCULATING THE CORRECT DOSE OF A HUMAN NONPRESCRIPTION MEDICATION FOR A DOG

—

Dog doses and human doses are not the same. The dose of a human drug for a dog must be calculated on the basis of the dog's body weight.

—

1. **Weigh the dog.** The traditional method of a person weighing himself with and without the dog, then subtracting the difference, is sufficiently accurate for all but tiny puppies. Example: if an owner weighs 150 pounds alone and

175 pounds while holding his dog, the dog weighs 25 pounds.

2. Determine the amount of active ingredients in each unit of the medication. Federal law requires that this information be on the label. Example: A "regular" aspirin tablet contains 325 milligrams of active ingredient. An "extra-strength" aspirin tablet contains 500 milligrams of aspirin. A "children's" aspirin contains 80 milligrams.

3. Calculate the dose. The amount of a drug necessary to treat a dog is calculated as the milligrams of the drug required to treat each pound that the dog weighs. The dog's weight is measured in pounds or kilograms, and the dose is expressed in *milligrams per pound of body weight* or in *milligrams per kilogram of body weight.* For example, if the effective dose of a drug is 10 milligrams per pound of body weight, a 10-pound dog or puppy would receive 100 milligrams of the drug. If the effective dose of the same drug were to be expressed as 25 milligrams per kilogram instead of as 10 milligrams per pound, the dog that weighs 4.5 kilograms (about 10 lbs.) would receive 112 milligrams of the drug. For most drugs, the small difference in the dose as calculated using pounds instead of kilograms is unimportant; the dose of a drug is often given as a range (for example, 30 to 60 milligrams per pound of body weight of the patient).

Because there is so much variation in the weight of dogs, and because the smaller the patient, the more accurately the dose of a drug must be calculated, it is important to actually weigh a dog before calculating the dose of its medication. Remember, guidelines given for determining the dose of a human drug by the age of the patient (three to five years, for example) may be entirely inappropriate when using the drug for a dog.

Example: One regular aspirin (325 mg) is too much for

the 25-pound dog that needs 250 mg of aspirin. One half of an extra-strength aspirin (half of 500 mg) or three children's aspirins (three 80-mg tablets) approximates the correct dose for this dog.

Adult or child-strength medications?

For the purpose of calculating a dose of medication, adult human products are designed with the 100-to-200-pound human in mind. Few dogs weigh 100 pounds or more. Many dogs weigh less than one tenth that amount. When a drug is available in a usable children's form, it is more accurate to use the child's preparation than it is to try to divide the adult preparation into appropriate doses. The exception would be a drug that is available in adult form in tablets, but in children's form only in fruit-flavored syrup. It is much easier to administer half of a tablet in a piece of meat to a dog than it is to try to persuade a dog to accept a teaspoonful of flavored liquid without spitting out most of it.

Children's medications are often labeled with an appropriate dose for patients of a given age or weight. These figures are approximate for a human child:

AGE IN YEARS	WEIGHT IN POUNDS
2 to 4	30 to 35
4 to 6	36 to 45
6 to 9	46 to 65
9 to 12	66 to 85
Over 12 (adult)	85 to 150

For example, a medication that is labeled "for children two to four years of age" indicates a child of 30 to 35 pounds. Dogs that weigh less must receive a smaller dose.

Medications designed for human infants are more suitable for use in puppies and dogs of smaller breeds.

Dividing tablets

Tablets and caplets may be easily divided using a pill-splitting device in order to obtain the correct dosage for the dog's weight.

Capsules, which are a liquid or powder enclosed in flexible gelatin, cannot be divided and should not be used for dogs if the dose is not appropriate.

DETERMINE THE FREQUENCY OF ADMINISTRATION FOR THE DOG

The frequency of administration for some drugs is vastly different for dogs than it is for humans. Example: Aspirin is given every eight hours to a dog, while ibuprofen is given to a dog only once every twenty-four to forty-eight hours. If ibuprofen is the drug selected, the dog should be given a dose only once a day to once every other day.

Check the drug label to determine if there are any side effects from the drug or limitations on the length of time that the drug should be used.

Medications to be applied to the skin

There is seldom a problem calculating the dose of a human topical preparation for use on a dog. The directions on the container will specify "apply a thin film," "apply liberally to affected area," or similar instructions. A few products state that an application should not exceed a given amount or that the medication should not be used more often than a stated interval. In such cases, the restrictions that apply to humans also apply to dogs.

For the purposes of human topical medication applied in a dog's eye or ear, it is safe to assume that a dog's eye is approximately the same size as a human's; a dog's ear canal is larger. If too large a quantity of these preparations is used, the excess is merely wasted.

Medications for prolonged or continuous use

Dogs with chronic medical conditions often require medication on a continuous basis. Just as with medication for human chronic conditions, some drugs can be used daily, some intermittently, and some drugs are dangerous if used for a long period of time.

• *Analgesics* may be used daily for chronic pain. An example is the dog with chronic arthritis caused by hip dysplasia. Though few studies have been done on the long-term use of nonprescription analgesics in the dog, the data acquired from human studies suggest that some analgesics such as aspirin can be used daily for years, but that other drugs might cause damage to the patient's liver or other organs. Where applicable, warnings are printed on the package. If an analgesic is to be used for more than a few days, the safest drug that is effective must be used at the lowest possible dose.

• *Laxatives* have use in the treatment of occasional constipation in humans and dogs. A need for laxatives on a continuous basis for either species indicates that a dietary change is in order.

• Some medications for treating the eye must be instilled on a regular basis. An example of these is drops for *glaucoma* and *keratitis sicca*. Diseases such as these cannot be cured, but can be controlled by faithful application of the medication several times a day.

• Drugs for application on the skin are intended to be used at regular intervals. Some flea medications, for example, are labeled to be used once a month. The stated intervals indicate the minimum length of time that the drug is effective.

Even if the problem is severe, the drugs should not be used more often than indicated on the package. If the drug is not effective at the labeled dose, a different treatment should be used. *Caution:* some flea medications are not safe for use with other drugs. Such warnings are printed on the label.

These standard abbreviations *are used in the charts in this book.*

> *Capsule:* cap.
> *Milligram:* mg
> *Tablet:* tab.
> *Tablespoonful:* tbs.
> *Teaspoonful:* tsp.

A nonstandard abbreviation used is **b.w.,** which stands for the **body weight** of the dog in pounds. For example, a medication that is administered at one tablet for every 10 pounds the dog weighs is abbreviated **1 per 10 lb b.w.**

5

HOW TO ADMINISTER MEDICATION
TO A DOG

The best medicine in the world is worthless unless the patient takes it. If you cannot get your dog to swallow the drug or allow you to apply medication to its skin, you might as well save your time and money.

Some dogs are more easily given medicine than others; some challenge the most determined owner to *make* them take any strange substance or to allow anything to be applied to them. Here are a few tricks that will make medicating your dog a relatively simple and painless process.

ADMINISTERING SOLID MEDICATION TO YOUR DOG:
TABLETS, CAPSULES, CAPLETS, AND GRANULES

Tablets or capsules
There are two methods of giving your dog a tablet or a capsule:

1. Open the dog's mouth and poke the medicine down its throat.
2. Hide the medicine in a tasty piece of food. With this second method, you do not have to manhandle the dog. You do not have to risk being bitten, accidentally or on purpose. You can make taking its medicine a pleasant experience for your dog.

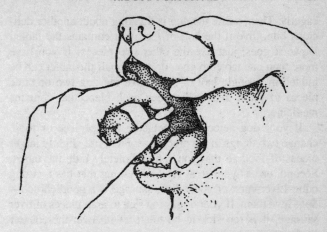

Administering a tablet.

Never mix tablets or caplets with a dog's whole meal. You will probably find the medicine left on the bottom of the bowl. *Never* give medication with the dog's usual diet unless your dog is such a greedy eater that it will gobble anything. If possible, give the dog its medicine before its regular dinner, when the dog is hungry and looking forward to eating.

Select some sort of food that is really a treat for your dog: hamburger meat, canned cat food, or a slice of frankfurter are all good choices. If your dog loves cheese, use that. If it relishes poultry, use a piece of boiled or roasted chicken. Select a food that the dog seldom gets and that it really wants.

Form three or four little balls of the treat food, each ball about half the size of a marshmallow. In one of these balls, include the tablet. Be sure the medication is completely surrounded by the treat. Remember which ball of food contains the tablet.

Give the dog a piece of the treat that *does not* contain the medication. The dog will eat it with relish. Give it another piece without medication; the dog will grab it and swallow eagerly. Then, while the dog is thinking about another delicious bite, give it the ball of food that contains the tablet. Down it goes, just like the other two pieces! If you have more than one tablet to give, or if only half the tablet can be hidden in a single ball of food, give the dog two or three pieces of plain treat in between each piece that contains medicine.

If your dog detects the medicine in the piece of food, change two things in the procedure: First, use slightly larger pieces of food so that you can completely hide the tablet. Second, use as your treat food something that has a strong odor. Liverwurst or goose-liver sausage is a good choice— dogs love them. If your dog is too sick to grab pieces of liver sausage, it is too sick to be treated with over-the-counter medication. Take it to your veterinarian.

Chewable tablets

Some veterinary products are marketed as chewable, and work very well. Most dogs will eat them. The medication in chewable tablets is more effective when it is chewed into small pieces before it enters the stomach.

Human chewable tablets usually do not have a flavor unpleasant to dogs; however, if your dog refuses to chew a tablet, place the tablet on a piece of paper and crush it with the back of a spoon. Sprinkle the crushed tablet onto some tasty food.

If you decide that you *must* force the medicine down your dog's throat without giving it in food, here is how to do it:

- Open the dog's mouth by surrounding its upper jaw with one hand and pulling its lower jaw down with the other hand. Have the tablet or caplet in the hand that opens the lower jaw (the right hand for a right-handed person).
- Pop the tablet into the dog's mouth *behind* the base of its tongue. If you do not get the medicine back into the

dog's throat, the dog will spit it out as soon as it is able.

- Quickly close the dog's mouth and hold it closed for a second. Rub the dog's nose, blow into its nose, or hold your fingers over its nostrils. Most of the time, this will force the dog to swallow.

- In many cases, the fourth step is to pick the tablet up off the floor and try again. Many medications will start to dissolve when they get wet with the dog's saliva. Dissolving tablets will taste terrible and will be even harder to give. Administering drugs in pieces of food is much easier for owners and much more pleasant for dogs.

ADMINISTERING LIQUID ORAL MEDICINE: *DROPS, SYRINGEFULS, SPOONFULS, OR DOSAGE CUPFULS*

Many human OTC oral medicines, especially those intended for infants and children, are supplied in liquid form. These usually include flavoring to enhance their acceptance by young human patients, but as very few dogs like bubble gum, grape, or fruit flavors, if you are going to administer human liquid medicines to your dog, you will probably have to do it forcefully. If possible, obtain liquid medicines designed for dogs. These products have flavors that dogs accept.

Dropperfuls
Children's drugs intended to be administered in small amounts usually are supplied in bottles with a calibrated medicine dropper in the top of the bottle. Vitamins and some children's pain and fever medication are supplied this way.

Calculate the dose by reading the label directions and interpreting them to fit the size and age of your dog. Shake the bottle to be sure the medicine is distributed through the fluid.

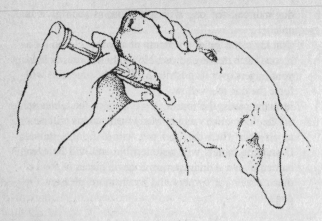

Administering liquid medication with a syringe.

Draw the desired dose into the medicine dropper. There usually is a line on the dropper indicating its contents in cubic centimeters (cc) so you can measure the correct dose. Open your dog's mouth and squirt the liquid onto its tongue. That is all there is to it.

Drugs given by the dropperful are usually too small a volume to be accidentally introduced into the lungs of even a small dog. The volume is also usually too small for a dog to easily spit out. Some of these medications are administered in small enough volumes to be incorporated in a piece of treat food, such as mixed with ground beef.

Syringefuls, spoonfuls, or dosage cupfuls

Some OTC liquid medications are supplied in bottles with an accompanying plastic cup to measure the dose. Some recommend that the dose be measured with standard measuring spoons. Most of these medications are formulated for human adults and contain flavoring even more obnoxious to dogs than fruit or bubble gum. Your veterinarian can furnish you with a 5- or 10-cc disposable syringe that may make giving a liquid medication less difficult. Administer only small amounts between swallows, as discussed above.

If you force too great a volume of any liquid into a dog's mouth, you may cause one or both of these two unpleasant occurrences:

1. You accidentally introduce some or all of the medicine into the dog's trachea (windpipe). If this happens, the dog will cough violently in an attempt to expel the foreign material. If enough liquid is introduced into the trachea, some may enter and cause damage to the dog's lungs.

2. More commonly, the dog will refuse to swallow immediately and will spit a portion of the medicine out of its mouth. Not only does this make a mess, but it makes it impossible to determine exactly how much of the medicine the dog actually swallowed. The dose your dog received could be inadequate; the dose actually could be almost zero. If you try to estimate how much was lost and give the dog some more of the preparation, you risk overdosing your dog.

Many OTC drugs useful in canine medicine that are supplied in liquids are also supplied in solid form. When available, the tablets or caplets are a much better choice—they are more easily and accurately administered to dogs than are the same drugs in liquid form.

MEDICINES APPLIED TO THE SKIN

It seems simple—just squeeze some out of the tube or scoop some out of the jar and smear it on the dog's affected area. Actually, you will have much better results from the use of OTC topical medications if you apply them carefully and correctly.

Follow these simple steps for the best results:

Restrain your dog

Dogs in pain misbehave because they fear more pain will be inflicted on their injured parts. They resist their owner's handling of the affected areas. Nothing an owner can do will convince a dog that the application of medication will make its injury better.

You cannot treat a dog while it is jumping around, struggling, or even trying to bite in self-defense. To treat a dog, it must be under control. You know your own dog; you know just how much restraint is necessary to medicate it.

Before you start to touch your dog's affected area, snap on its leash. The leash is a symbol of authority to a dog; the leash indicates that you can restrain its movements.

Have a friend or assistant help you hold the dog. The assistant should hold the dog on a short leash or, if necessary, hold the dog by the loose skin of its neck just behind each of the dog's ears. Under no circumstances should the assistant ever

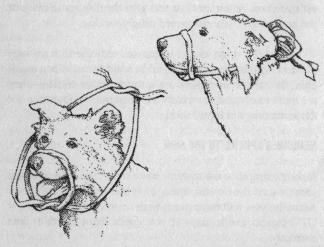

Applying a muzzle with a soft cord. The muzzle must be fitted snugly if the dog is to be prevented from biting.

loosen his or her grip until you have completed your treatment. If the dog obeys you better than it obeys any other person, you can hold it and ask your assistant to apply the medicine.

If you think that your dog might try to bite when it is treated, muzzle it. Muzzles can be purchased at pet supply stores. Use a nylon cone muzzle if possible. When fitted properly, these muzzles are safe for the handler and comfortable for the dog. If you do not have a cone muzzle, in many cases, the nylon device called a "head halter" available at pet shops will provide enough restraint to keep you from being bitten *if* an assistant keeps tension on the leash.

Clean the affected area

The dog will gain no benefit from medication applied over dirt, crusts, and matted hair. Before you apply medication, you must first cleanse the area.

Wash the area. Use a clean washcloth to gently lather the affected area with warm water and mild soap. Do not scrub—soak off dirt and grime with lots of water. Be sure to rinse away all of the soap.

If you must cleanse a large area on your dog, stand the dog in a tub and use a hose attachment to rinse it. If you have no hose, you can pour several containers of clean, warm water over the area. Blot away the water with a clean bath towel.

Remove crusts and old scabs. During your cleansing routine, remove whatever is adhering to your dog's injured areas. Always remove scabs if infection could be lurking underneath them. To soften scabs, hold a cotton ball soaked in warm water to the affected areas. If the scabs are dry and tightly adhered to the underlying tissue, several minutes and two or three wet cotton balls may be required to soften the scabs enough to loosen them.

When the scabs are soft, wipe them away with a clean cotton ball. Roll the edges of large scabs from the outside of the wound toward the center. You may use tweezers to lift the edges of the soft scabs.

Do not hesitate to remove every bit of the dirt and scabs. If you leave contaminated, dead tissue in an injured area, the body must eliminate it before healthy tissue can grow in its place.

Remove hair if necessary. You may have to clip the hair away from your dog's sore places. If you have no clippers, you can use scissors to *carefully* cut the hair so that medication can be applied directly to the skin. There is always the danger of cutting the dog with scissors, so never snip unless you are absolutely sure that you are not snipping skin.

How to apply medicine to the skin

Lotions are thick liquids that are designed to be applied to skin. To apply lotions, pump (or squirt) them on, and rub them in. If you select lotions that contain a fragrance, your dog may be repelled by the odor and not lick the lotion off immediately.

Cremes are very much like thick lotions. The term *vanishing creme* means that the creme vanishes when it is rubbed into the skin. Cremes can be squeezed out of a tube and rubbed onto the skin when a barrier between the skin and the air is not desired.

Ointments are thick and greasy, intended to cover, protect, and medicate injured areas. Ointments are intended to contact the skin but not to be rubbed in. Spread ointments liberally. You may use some ointments under bandages.

Powders for topical application to wounds are usually supplied in "puffer" bottles. To apply wound powders, do just as the description states: take off the cap and squeeze the container, "puffing" the medication onto the affected area. Since you do not have to touch the dog to apply medication from a puffer, this form of treatment is well tolerated by dogs.

Insecticide Powders are intended to kill parasites in a dog's coat. "Flea" powders are usually sold in shaker cans. You must apply the powder to the skin, not just to the surface of the hair. It is important to shake the powder over the entire dog. Remember to roll the dog over and to cover its underside with the powder as well as its back and head.

Liquid wound sprays are applied by first shaking the container, then pointing the nozzle at the affected area and depressing the button. Many dogs are startled at the sound and the cold feeling of sprays, so ask your assistant to restrain the dog before you spray. This will help avoid the dog jumping away and the spray landing in the wrong place.

Liquid flea and tick sprays must be sprayed on the entire dog, including its underside, in order to control the parasites. These sprays must contact the dog's skin as well as its hair in order to work properly. Have an assistant restrain your dog until you get the whole job done.

Insecticide Dips are used to kill external parasites. In theory, the dip medication is mixed with water and the dog immersed in the solution. In reality, few of us want to prepare a large enough container of medicine in which to completely immerse our dogs.

Dips are equally as effective when they are sponged thoroughly into a dog's coat. If you prepare a gallon of dip, you can sponge several short-haired dogs or a couple of long-haired ones. Stand the dog in a tub or pan to catch the solution that drips off. Soak up the solution in the pan with your sponge and squeeze it out of the sponge onto another part of the dog. You will be surprised how many dogs can be treated with one gallon of dip!

One-spot flea medications are designed to be applied to the dog's skin in a single area. These products are usually applied on an area that the dog cannot lick—the back of the neck or between the shoulder blades. The medications work by being absorbed by the dog's skin. *All* of the medication must be placed on the skin; any that contacts only the dog's hair will not be absorbed. Part the hair to expose an adequate area of skin before you snip open the package containing the medicine. If your dog has a thick coat, you may want to snip off and inconspicuous amount of hair to be sure that every bit of the medicine contacts its skin.

———

Most nonprescription medications are relatively harmless to the patient, even if applied in excessive quantities. Take care to keep all medications not designed for opthalmic use out of your dog's eyes. If you must apply a medication on the skin near an eye, cover the eye with one hand while you apply the medication with the other.

———

What if my dog licks the stuff?

When drugs for humans are formulated, manufacturers do not have to consider the consequences if their patients lick the medication off their skins. Humans seldom lick their wounds. When drugs are formulated for use on dogs, the possibility that the patient will lick the medication is an important consideration.

Almost every dog will instinctively lick any injured area that is within reach of its tongue. Licking serves very important functions in the healing of wounds and abrasions on dogs.

- Licking removes dirt, dead tissue, and scabs under which bacteria can thrive.
- Licking keeps the damaged area moist. New cells cannot grow over dry, desiccated areas of skin.

You should not, and probably cannot, prevent your dog from licking its unmedicated wounds. Nature instructs a dog to remove irritants from its body. On the other hand, when a dog licks off medicine, that medication is no longer present to help heal the wound. More important, medicine that a dog accidentally swallows may make it sick.

Dogs can lick every part of their bodies except their heads, necks, and the top of their shoulders. If you are applying medication to any other area, be careful! Follow these tips to minimize your dog's licking of its medication:

Select skin medications that are absorbed by the skin. "Vanishing" cremes are intended to be absorbed into the skin, whereas ointments are designed to provide a protective barrier on top of the skin. When rubbed into a dog's skin, an antibiotic creme cannot be licked off as completely as can a greasy ointment. A liquid medication that dries on the skin will still be effective if a dog licks it.

Distract your dog for a few minutes after you apply medication to its skin. Feed your dog. Take your dog for a walk. Play ball with it. Take its attention away from the medicated area to allow the medicine to be absorbed before the dog has the opportunity to lick it. If you are bathing or dipping your dog in a medication, prevent the dog from licking its coat until it is dry.

Use topical medications designed for dogs when possible. Manufacturers of drugs for dogs take into consideration that almost all dogs will lick medicine off their skins. For this reason, drugs formulated for dogs' skin seldom contain ingredients that are toxic to dogs in recommended amounts.

Read every label. Look for these words: **DO NOT TAKE INTERNALLY.** If this or any similar phrase appears on a medication, never use it on your dog in an area where it can be licked off and swallowed. If you have the slightest doubt about the safety of a medicine, consult your veterinarian or the local poison control center before you apply it to your dog.

APPLYING MEDICINE IN THE EYE

Anything *seriously* wrong with an eye is a job for your veterinarian. However, you may have an occasion to apply ointment or drops in your dog's eyes for minor irritations.

Every injured eye is extremely painful. When applying

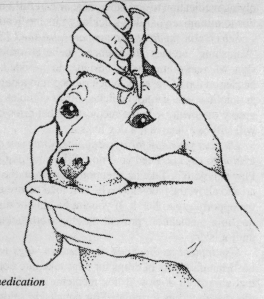

*Applying medication
to the eye.*

medication in an eye, the person restraining the dog does
most of the work. Eye drops and eye ointments are supplied
in tiny squeeze bottles, dropper bottles, or very small tubes.
The contents of these containers are sterile, so in order to
prevent contamination, it is important to get the medication
in the eye without touching the bottle, the dropper, or the tip
of the tube to the surface of the eye.

1. The assistant should take a firm hold of the dog's loose
skin just behind each of its ears. The assistant holds the dog
with its muzzle pointing slightly upwards.

2. The person applying the medicine gently pulls the dog's
lower lid down with one hand. With the other hand, she
holds the container at least ½ inch above the eye. She rests

her hand holding the medicine on the dog's forehead, so if the dog moves, the medicine container will move with it. She drops the liquid or ointment preparation directly onto the dog's cornea (transparent front part of the eyeball) without touching the container to the eye itself. It may take a few trials before the medicine goes into the eye and not onto the dog's nose.

If the container touches the eye, the dog's eye may be damaged and the container will become contaminated. Keep the container more than ½ inch above the eye until you have practiced and know that you can control the situation. It is better to waste a few drops of medication than to jab your dog in the eye.

Eye ointment can be applied as a small strip of medication squeezed out of the tube into the *inner surface* of the dog's lower eyelid. When the dog blinks, the ointment will be spread over the surface of its eye. Make sure not to touch the dog with the tip of the tube.

APPLYING MEDICINE IN THE EAR

It is of little value to put medicine in a dog's ear when the ear is full of pus, scabs, or wax. Many conditions of dogs' ears are so painful that veterinarians will have to administer sedatives to the dogs to be able to properly clean debris out of their ears.

When your dog's affected ears are clean, you need only to drop or squirt the required amount of medication into its ear canals. If the ears are not clean, you may have to remove old debris and old medication before each application of new medication. Your helper should restrain the dog just as for medication applied to its eye while you clean the ear with a cotton ball and apply the new dose of ear medicine.

Infected ears are often so painful that dogs vigorously resist any attempt by owners to apply ear medicine. If the owner gives up and does not persist in applying the medication, the dog's ears will not get better. When your dog struggles to prevent you from touching its sore ears, remember: you are doing this for its own good. If you cannot medicate the ears yourself, get veterinary assistance until the ears have become less painful.

APPLYING BANDAGES

Bandaging the body

Bandages are occasionally applied to a dog's body to keep the dog from chewing or licking an affected area. *Never* wrap tape around your dog's chest or abdomen. *Never* cover the dog's body with a tube of cloth. You will soon find that the dog has scratched the wrap into a narrow band just in front of its hips, where the bandage will only irritate the dog.

If you must apply a covering to your dog's body, use a T-shirt. Use an adult size for a big dog, a child size for a medium dog, and an infant size for a toy breed. Stick the dog's front legs into the arms of the T-shirt and its head through the neck opening. Cut three holes in appropriate places for the dog's back legs and tail. Yes, the shirt will be baggy underneath the dog's chest and below its tail. You could sew up the excess material, or just let it hang there. Use safety pins only if you can watch to be sure the dog does not try to eat its covering.

Bandaging the limbs

Most bandaging of dogs is done to the legs and paws. Most dogs chew the bandages off as fast as their owners apply them, because bandages are irritating. In the vast majority of cases, the injury will get better far more quickly if not bandaged at all.

It is very difficult to keep a bandaged paw dry. Wet bandages on paws are an excellent place for bad organisms to grow—if you do not believe this, smell a bandaged paw. After a day or so, it will smell like rotten meat. Of course, a dog that licks an injured foot removes the medicine you apply, but the dog also licks off dirt and bacteria. Nature shows the dog how to keep the area clean.

If you must bandage a paw and the bandage may become wet, protect it with a plastic bag. NEVER hold the plastic bag onto the paw with a rubber band; use a piece of tape.

—

IMPORTANT: Never bandage a paw tightly enough to cut off circulation. If blood cannot circulate through the dog's tissues, the cells will die. Gangrene may result.

—

Never apply a bandage to a leg above the paw without including the paw in the bandage. The paw below the bandage will swell up if the circulation is impaired.

Bandaging the tip of the tail—occasionally a good idea

Many short-haired, long-tailed dogs swing their tails around so vigorously that they damage the skin on the tips of their tails. Bird-hunting dogs and Great Danes are especially prone to this kind of injury. These dogs can have chronically bleeding tail tips when they constantly thrash their tails through thick underbrush. It became popular to dock the tails of some breeds of hunting dogs to eliminate this problem. All the German pointing breeds—German shorthaired pointer, vizsla, Weimaraner, and others—have docked tails. The problem even exists in some breeds that are not short-haired. Spaniels all are docked at birth.

Applying a bandage to the end of a dog's tail sometimes is a good idea. It is easy to do.

1. Go to the nearest discount store and buy a couple of pairs of cheap cotton gloves.
2. Cut the fingers off the gloves. You will have ten little cotton fingers from each pair. Throw away the remainder of the gloves.

3. Place a cloth finger over the dog's injured tail tip. Attach the cloth to the dog's hair with silver duct tape. Use plenty of tape and stick it only to the hair. *Never* make it tight.

4. When the cloth finger becomes damaged, replace it with another one. The duct tape will pull off easily. If the glove finger falls off the tail when the dog wags, you did not use a wide enough band of tape.

PART II

THE USE OF NONPRESCRIPTION DRUGS IN THE DOG

6

THE EYE

Pharmacy shelves are loaded with over-the-counter preparations designed for use in the human eye. Pet shops and feed stores have similar (in some cases, identical) products for use in dogs. Are these drugs effective? Could they be harmful?

The answers to the above questions are both *yes* and *no*. If used correctly and for the correct conditions, these products are completely adequate. If used incorrectly or used as a substitute for needed veterinary attention, the use of nonprescription drugs in the eye could complicate or delay proper therapy and allow existing conditions to get worse. If eye problems are misdiagnosed or treated incorrectly, the consequences to the patient may be severe and painful.

—

A Look Into the Canine Eye

- The *cornea* is the transparent structure on the front of the eyeball.
- The *iris* is the circular, colored membrane behind the cornea.
- The *pupil* is the opening in the center of the iris through which light passes.
- The *sclera* is the "white" of the eye.
- The *nictitating membrane* is the dog's "third eyelid." This membrane is located at the inside corner of the eye. Its function is to partly cover and protect the eyeball.
- The *conjunctiva* is the tissue covering the sclera and lining the inside of the eyelids.
- The *lacrimal glands* produce the tears that keep the eye moist.

• The *lens* is the spherical body within the eye that directs rays of light onto the retina.

———

SIGNS OF EYE PROBLEMS

The signs of many eye problems are very similar. The patient evidences pain by squinting and pawing at its eye; it avoids strong light and shrinks away from anyone touching its head. The sclera is pinkish or red and a thick, crusty discharge is present, often sticking the lids together.

In all but the most minor cases involving the eye, a veterinarian should make the initial diagnosis and recommend treatment. Only if the condition is one that will respond to nonprescription drugs should the owner continue treatment with nonprescription medications.

Medications for use in the eye that contain antibiotics or steroids are available by prescription only. Such medications are designed for serious conditions of the eye, conditions that cannot be diagnosed accurately by nonmedical personnel. Over-the-counter nonprescription medications are useful for appropriate minor eye irritation in both the human and canine species. Every human pharmacy and every pet shop has a display of these products.

———

Nonprescription drugs should not be used to substitute for professional diagnosis and treatment of serious opthalmic conditions

———

CONGENITAL DEFECTS OF THE EYE AND EYELIDS

Abnormal eyelashes

Trichiasis is a condition in which the abnormal lashes grow inward. *Districhiasis* occurs when two eyelashes grow from a single follicle. The extra lash often is in a damaging position. *Ectopic cilia* are eyelashes that grow in the wrong places.

Signs: Painful eyes. The affected dog squints and avoids bright light. Watery or thick discharge from one or both eyes. The cornea may appear cloudy or damaged.

Affected dogs: Puppies and young dogs. Pekingese, poodle, and Bedlington terrier breeds often have this condition.

Treatment: Surgical removal of the abnormal lashes is the only permanent remedy. Temporary relief is obtained by plucking the offending eyelashes. The lashes will grow back in the same abnormal position.

Medication: Only after removal of the lashes, the damaged eye may be treated with Terramycin Opthalmic Ointment Veterinary. Contents: oxytetracycline hydrochloride and polymixin B sulfate. How supplied: ⅛-ounce tubes. Dose: apply in eye(s) every six to eight hours. Availability: pet shops and pet supply catalogs.

Corneal pigmentation
Certain breeds of dogs apparently have a genetic tendency to develop blood vessels, pigment deposits, and groups of cells on the surface of the cornea. The condition occurs most often in German shepherd dogs. These abnormal masses limit the transparency of the cornea. If the masses become extensive, the dog's vision will be severely limited. To be treated successfully, these cases require veterinary attention.

Ectropion
This condition affects the lower eyelid.

Signs: The lid droops down and forms a pocket below the eye. Foreign matter that accumulates under the drooping lower lid of affected dogs can cause irritation and infection.

Affected dogs: The normal bloodhound eye is an example of ectropion. Ectropion often affects other breeds such as the basset, bulldog, cocker spaniel, and St. Bernard.

Treatment: Regular cleansing of the eye, flushing away foreign matter if needed, and the application of protective eye ointment can handle most cases of ectropion. Surgery to remove the excess lower eyelid skin may be necessary in severe cases.

Medication: "Eye wash," "eye rinse," or "eye flush" solutions. These products are used to rid the eye of foreign material and debris. Most of the products on the market are intended for canine rather than human use. An eye wash is a buffered normal saline solution with or without eye antiseptics such as boric acid. The products are intended only to flush away debris in the eye. Since they contain no "drug" in the legal sense, their contents are not always stated on the label. Sterile gauze squares moistened with these solutions are called "eye wipes." These are available to clean the areas surrounding dogs' eyes, including skin folds below the eye. Cotton balls moistened by the owner with the product serve the same purpose.

Lavoptik is a product intended for humans. It is supplied in a 6-ounce bottle with an eye cup. It can be applied to dogs' eyes with a dropper or from a plastic squeeze bottle. Lavoptik is difficult to use on dogs without contaminating the solution.

Opticlear is also a human product. The plastic squeeze bottle is easily used on the dog's eye.

Entropion

In this condition, the lower or both the upper and lower eyelids are turned inward so that the eyelashes rub against the

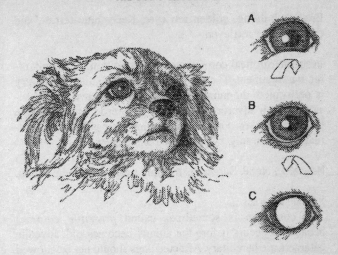

Normal and abnormal eyes. (A) Entropion. *The lower lid turns in, allowing the lashes to rub the eyeball. (B)* Ectropion. *The lower lid turns out away from the eye. (C)* Senile cataract.

cornea. In the worst cases of entropion, the layers of the cornea become damaged by the constant rubbing of the lashes. If the damage is very deep, the cornea may perforate and the eye may be destroyed.

Signs: Entropion is present at birth and can be detected soon after puppies' eyes open. In most cases, both eyes are affected, but not necessarily to the same degree. Dogs with entropion have a permanent squint, occular discharge, and evidence of pain.

Affected dogs: Entropion can occur in any breed of dog, but it is very common in exophthalmic dogs (with bulging eyes) such as the Pekingese and the Lhasa apso. Entropion is so common as to be considered "normal" in the Shar-pei. Other breeds that are often affected are the Chow Chow,

English bulldog, golden retriever, Kerry blue terrier, and the Labrador retriever.

Treatment: Surgical correction of the condition is the only effective treatment. The earlier in a pup's life that the surgery is performed, the more likely the pup is to have normal vision. In their advertisements, Shar-pei breeders often include the phrase "eyes done," meaning that their puppies have already had the surgery performed on their eyelids.

Medication: None. Surgery is the only treatment for entropion.

Juvenile cataract

The condition is sometimes called *presenile cataract* because it occurs before the animal becomes old. Juvenile cataracts are hereditary. Affected dogs should not be allowed to reproduce and pass the trait to their offspring.

Signs: A white or gray cloudy mass can be seen deep in the eye. The normally clear lens of the eye becomes opaque. This mass should not be mistaken for a cloudy cornea, which is on the outer surface of the eye.

In juvenile cataract, the opacity of the lens may be complete. Vision in these eyes is severely limited. Dogs with juvenile cataract develop this condition before the dogs are three years old, long before they would develop cataracts from natural aging.

Affected dogs: May occur in any breed. Common in poodles, cocker spaniels, wirehaired terriers, miniature schnauzers, Boston terriers, and Afghan hounds.

Treatment: No medicine will alleviate this condition. Surgical removal of the affected lens is the only method of restoring vision to severely affected dogs.

Because of the structure of the canine eye, cataract surgery is more difficult in dogs than it is in humans. All in-traoccular surgery (surgery within the eye), including cataract surgery, requires the special training and special equipment of a veterinary opthalmologist.

Is this surgery necessary? Only the owner can judge if the dog is so handicapped as to be disabled by its loss of vision. If the dog can function reasonably well, surgery for juvenile cataract is often not recommended.

AGE-RELATED PROBLEMS OF THE EYE

Glaucoma

Glaucoma occurs more frequently in humans than it does in dogs, and is caused by an increase of pressure within the eye. If not treated correctly, a dog (or a human) with glau-coma will become blind.

Signs: One or both eyes may be affected. If the condition ap-pears in one eye, it is very likely to appear in the other.

The condition is always painful. An eye affected by glau-coma may appear to be bulging. The cornea is cloudy and the pupils are widely dilated. The "blink reflex" (in which the patient blinks in response to a threat to its eye) will be absent, and often the cornea is completely insensitive to touch.

Affected animals: Most commonly the American cocker spaniel. Females are affected more often than males. A hereditary tendency toward this condition is obvious.

Treatment: Glaucoma in dogs can be treated with surgery and/or medication. If the condition is diagnosed before the eye becomes sightless, vision usually can be saved. In dogs, glaucoma is most often treated with drops that must be ap-plied in the eye several times a day. The results depend on the owners' compliance. If the medication is administered faithfully, the dog's vision and comfort can be maintained.

Any dog with a cloudy, insensitive cornea and diminished vision should be seen by a veterinary opthalmologist without delay. The earlier in the course of the disease that treatment is started, the more likely it is that the dog's vision will be preserved. Glaucoma in dogs is usually treated with eye drops that cause and maintain constriction of the pupil. The drops must be applied at regular intervals several times a day. Some cases of canine glaucoma can be helped by surgical treatment that can only be performed by a veterinary opthalmologist.

Medication: Both human and canine glaucoma are treated with eye drops that are available by prescription only.

Keratitis sicca

Keratitis refers to an inflammation of the cornea. *Sicca* means dry. In both humans and dogs, this condition is referred to as "dry eye." The lacrimal glands fail to produce tears, the natural lubricant of the eye. Eventually the cornea becomes dry and damaged.

Signs: The conjunctiva is inflamed. The cornea may be ulcerated. A thick, sticky discharge often is present. The patient demonstrates pain by rubbing its eyes and avoiding bright lights. The condition generally affects both eyes equally.

Keratitis sicca is considered to be a disease of middle and old age. The condition is rare in puppies, in which it is probably a congenital abnormality of the lacrimal glands.

Treatment: Keratitis sicca can be controlled but not cured. Treatment of the condition can be very successful if the owner of an affected dog is willing to apply medication in the dog's eyes several times a day. The treatment must be continued throughout the life of the patient.

Medication: In both humans and dogs, nonprescription eye drops containing methylcellulose are used in the control of keratitis sicca. Many brands of "artificial tears" are on the market. Prescription medications containing additional drugs may be needed in the early stages of treatment if the condition is complicated by a bacterial infection. Of course, the condition must be diagnosed by a veterinarian before treatment is started. These common brand names of artificial tears can be used:

- COMFORT TEARS, ISOPTO-TEARS, LACRIL. Contents: methylcellulose formulas.
- DRY EYE THERAPY. Contents: glycerine formula.
- LACRI-LUBE. Contents: petrolatum formula.

Senile cataract

In both dogs and humans, cataract formation is an inevitable result of aging in both humans and dogs. As an animal ages, the normally clear lens gradually becomes opaque, a cataract forms, and vision is impaired. The term *senile cataract* denotes that the lens opacity is related to age; the term does not indicate that the patient is senile.

Signs: The cataract appears as a gray or white round object commonly seen within the eye of most dogs over about eight years of age. The age at which a cataract forms is probably determined by the dog's heredity.

A *mature cataract* is one in which the lens has become completely opaque. No light can pass through the lens to the retina, and the eye is sightless. Cataracts of most dogs do not become completely mature. The dog's vision is diminished, but most dogs' eyes with a cataract do not become sightless.

Cataract formation in older dogs is frequently accompanied by degeneration of the retina. If the retina is damaged, sight will not be restored even if the cataract is surgically removed. Only a specialist who uses special electronic equipment can do clinical testing of the retina. If the results of the test show retinal degeneration, surgical removal of the lens will not restore the affected animal's sight.

Treatment: Although some lens abnormalities in young dogs have been said to respond to vitamin A therapy, treatment of senile cataracts with ointments or dietary additives is entirely ineffective.

EYE PROBLEMS RELATED TO INJURY

Conjunctivitis

The tissue covering the sclera ("white" of the eye) and lining the lids is the *conjunctiva*. An inflammation of this tissue is *conjunctivitis*.

Common causes of conjunctivitis are dust and other particles that enter the eye accidentally. This frequently happens to dogs that are allowed to ride with their heads out of car windows. The condition may affect one or both eyes.

Signs: At first the affected eye will water as the lacrimal glands produce tears to wash away the irritating material. The discharge from the eye will become thick and sticky. Blood vessels in the sclera may become prominent, causing the eye to appear reddened. A dog with conjunctivitis may have evidence of pain and photophobia (sensitivity to light).

Treatment: Simple cases of conjunctivitis are treated successfully by flushing the eye with a sterile solution sold for human use and treating the irritated conjunctival membranes with a bland ointment such as an OTC human product. If the condition persists, an infection may be present or foreign material may still be in the eye. A veterinarian should examine these cases.

Medication: Eye washes as used for cases of ectropion. Terramycin opthalmic ointment may be applied after the eye is cleaned.

"Red eye" caused by blunt trauma

If a dog receives a blow to its eyeball, blood vessels in the conjunctiva or underlying sclera may burst.

Signs: Blood spots covering all or part of the white of the dog's eye. If the damage is not severe, the eye will not be painful. Normally only the injured eye will be affected. If occular discharge is present, it will be slight.

Treatment: Just as with a human "black eye," a dog's "red eye" will take time to disappear. The red spots on the conjunctiva will gradually discolor, then fade as the blood is absorbed. The entire process will take two weeks or more. Treatment is not needed unless the eye is painful, eye discharge is present, the dog squints, or the dog rubs its eye. If any of these conditions is present, the diagnosis may be incorrect and a veterinarian should be consulted.

Traumatic keratitis (damage to the cornea)

Damage or irritation to the cornea (the transparent membrane at the front of the eye through which light passes) is called *traumatic keratitis*. This condition is much more serious and much more painful to the patient than is conjunctivitis. A common cause of traumatic keratitis is foreign material that enters the eye and scratches or penetrates the cornea.

Signs: Usually only one eye is affected. If left untreated, keratitis may result in permanent damage to the eye. Traumatic keratitis has a sudden onset. The first sign in the dog is pain. The patient will hold its eye closed and vigorously resist examination of the affected eye.

If the damage is severe enough to allow fluid to enter the tissue, the normally transparent cornea will appear to have a gray or bluish cloudy film. This film may cover the entire cornea or only part of it.

Treatment: The consequences of neglecting injuries to the cornea are so severe that treatment should not be attempted by anyone who is not a doctor. Since the condition is very painful to the patient, treatment should not be delayed.

Medication: Only prescription medications are effective.

—

A veterinarian who specializes in disease of the eye should be consulted in all serious cases involving the cornea.

—

EYE DISEASES CAUSED BY ALLERGIES, INFECTION, AND IRRITATION

Allergic conjunctivitis

Signs: The conjunctiva is reddened. The dog rubs or scratches at its eyes. The condition always affects both eyes at the same time.

Affected dogs: Any dog that comes in contact with a substance to which it is allergic, such as pollen. Wind-borne particles that are blown into the eyes when a dog is permitted to ride in a car with its head out of the window are a common cause of allergic conjunctivitis.

Treatment: Clean eyes with an eye wash, and instill drops of an antihistamine or vasoconstrictor solution.

Medication: These common brand names can be used:

• OCUHIST. Contents: pheniramine maleate with naphaxoline HCI. How supplied: 15-millileter dropper

bottles. Dose: One or two drops in each affected eye
every six hours.
- VISINE. Contents: tetrahydrolozine hydrochloride.
How supplied: 0.5-ounce dropper bottles. Dose: One
drop in each affected eye every six hours.

"Cherry Eye"

Signs: The common name of this condition comes from its
appearance: a red, cherrylike mass protrudes from the inside
corner of the affected dog's eye. This mass is composed of
irritated and swollen glands on the inner surface of the dog's
nictitating membrane.

Affected animals: Cherry eye can occur in dogs of all breeds
and ages; it is most common in young dogs of breeds that
have some degree of ectropion, such as the cocker spaniel.

Treatment: The application of opthalmic ointments may reduce the glandular swelling, but will not eliminate a cherry
eye. The only successful treatment is surgery.

Conjunctivitis caused by infection

Bacterial infections of the conjunctiva can occur alone or
following an eye irritation or injury caused by foreign material in the eye. Conjunctivitis that persists for more than a
few days has an underlying cause more serious than simple
irritation. Until the cause is discovered and treated appropriately, the condition will not disappear. The dog with significant discharge from the eyes that does not respond to cleaning and treatment with bland medications should have professional attention.

Tear staining in light-colored dogs

Signs: White or light-colored dogs are subject to developing
brown stains below the inner corner of each eye. Tear staining is caused by bacterial growth in the areas of the dog's

face that are constantly moist from tears overflowing from the eye. It occurs on dark-colored dogs as well as on light-colored ones, but the stain is not as apparent on dark hair. The condition is unattractive, although not harmful to the dog. Owners of white show dogs and many other owners object to the appearance of tear staining.

Treatment: The prevention and removal of the stains is not difficult to accomplish. If present, long hair should be clipped away from the stained areas to allow the moisture to evaporate and to keep the areas as dry as possible. Clipping should be repeated at two-week intervals.

Medication: The application of oxytetracycline (Terramycin) ointment inside the dog's lower eyelid once or twice a day will inhibit the growth of bacteria that thrive in the moist areas. When the stains have disappeared, application of the ointment may be needed only every other day.

Improvement of the appearance of a dog with a badly stained face will take ten days to two weeks; improvement in mild cases should be noticed within three or four days. The procedures must be carried out for the life of the dog to prevent the stain from returning.

7

THE EAR: INSIDE AND OUT

To a student of anatomy, the "ear" consists of the structures within the head. The part outside the head is called the auricle, ear flap, or pinna. *Otitis* signifies an inflammation of one or more of the structures of the ear inside the head. *Otitis externa* is an infection of the outer ear canal from the eardrum to the outside.

Only the outer ear canal is accessible for medicating. The structure of the middle and inner ear are sealed off by the tympanic membrane. Rupture of the tympanic membrane or infection of the middle or inner ear is always a serious condition that requires expert medical attention.

—

A Look at the Canine Ear

- The *auricle* is the ear flap or "leather." It is also called the *pinna*.
- The *outer ear* is the ear canal from the eardrum to the outside opening.
- The *tympanic membrane* is the eardrum.
- The *middle ear* is the part just behind the eardrum. It contains the three bones of the ear and the opening to the Eustachian tube.
- The *inner ear* is the deepest structure of the ear. It contains the organs of balance and hearing.

—

MEDICINES FOR USE IN THE EAR

Dogs have far more ear problems than have humans. Both the lifestyle of the dog and the structure of the canine ear increase the susceptibility of dogs to infections by a variety of organisms, as well as to trauma of the external ear canal and the auricle.

The difference between prescription and nonprescription ear medications

Prescription medications contain specific antibiotic, antifungal, and anti-inflammatory agents, alone or in combination. These drugs are directed toward the control of specific microorganisms in the ear. These ear preparations can be purchased only with prescriptions from veterinarians.

Nonprescription medications contain substances not directed toward controlling specific microorganisms, but directed toward causing the ear canal to be an unfavorable site for microorganisms to grow. Almost all nonprescription human ear medications are intended only to dissolve earwax. Nonprescription canine ear preparations serve one or more of these functions: to *dissolve wax,* to *acidify,* to *dry,* to *disinfect,* and to *kill ear mites.*

Human Nonprescription Ear Preparations

DRUG	SOME BRAND NAMES	FUNCTION
Carbamate peroxide	DEBROX	softens wax
	MURINE EAR WAX REMOVAL SYSTEM	softens wax
Olive oil	SWEET OIL (generic)	softens wax
Hydrogen peroxide	Generic	softens wax

Canine nonprescription ear preparations

An enormous number and variety of products with which to treat dogs' ears are available as OTC preparations. Many of these products have only local or regional distribution and will not be available in every part of the United States. If a specific patented ear medication is not available, others containing the same or similar drugs are sure to be on the shelves of local pet stores.

It is the owners' responsibility to read the label on each product and to make informed choices about the medications that they select for their dogs.

Drugs Contained in Canine Nonprescription Ear Medications

DRUG	PURPOSE
Propylene glycol	dissolve earwax
Benzoic acid	acidify ear canal
Lactic acid	acidify ear canal
Malic acid	acidify ear canal
Salicylic acid	acidify ear canal
Voric acid, liquid and powder	acidify and dry ear canal
Carbamate peroxide	soften ear wax
Yucca, aloe, and other herbal extracts	appeal to owner
Rotenone	kill ear mites
Pyrethrins	kill ear mites
Isopropyl alcohol	inhibit microorganisms
Other antiseptics and disinfectants	inhibit microorganisms
Fragrances	appeal to owner

EAR INFECTIONS (OTITIS EXTERNA)

Otitis externa, infection of the outer ear, is caused by microorganisms that thrive in the warm, moist, nonacid environment of the dog's ear. Several types of organisms cause the condition; bacteria and yeast are the most common. Many ear infections contain both bacteria and yeast.

Signs: Wax and purulent discharge are produced by the lining of the ear canal in response to the irritation caused by the organisms. The dog may shake its head, scratch its ears, or cry when its ears are touched. A bad odor is often present.

Animals affected: Breeds with pendulous ears and breeds with excessive hair growth in the ear canals are especially susceptible to otitis externa. The condition is common in poodles, cocker spaniels, and basset hounds. The long ear flaps and the hair in the canals of these breeds do not permit air to circulate in the ears. The ear canals are always warm, moist, and dark—a perfect site for the growth of organisms.

Treatment: First, the ear canal must be cleaned and dried to discourage growth of microorganisms. The hair surrounding the external ear opening must be removed. In the case of long-eared, long-haired breeds, the hair on the entire underside of the ear should be clipped away at two-week intervals.

Many long-haired dogs have a great deal of hair growth inside their ear canals. This hair must also be removed to allow moisture to evaporate, to allow exudate to be cleaned out, and to allow medication to reach the site of the problem. Since this hair cannot be reached with a scissors or a clipper, it must be plucked out with forceps. In many cases, this procedure will be painful to the dog and must be done under anesthetic. The initial treatment of otitis externa often is a job for a veterinarian.

If a large amount of exudate is present in the infected ears, it must be removed by flushing the ear canal with an appropriate solution followed by swabbing with cotton-tipped applicators. Hardened wax should be softened by the use of a solvent for several days before the ears are flushed. When the ear canal is cleaned and dried, medications can be instilled that keep the ear canal acidified and that dissolve new wax as it forms.

Prevention of outer-ear infections

Regular hair removal, cleaning, and application of medication are needed to prevent ear infections from returning. Dogs that have had chronic outer-ear infections never should be considered "cured." The ears of such animals should be inspected and treated regularly.

Owners, especially owners of long-eared dogs, should inspect their animals' ears at least once a week. Long-haired dogs should have the undersides of their ears clipped and the hair removed from their ear canals as part of routine grooming procedures.

At the first sign of odor or discharge, treatment should be instituted. Ear infections are much easier to treat successfully before the condition becomes chronic.

Treatment of outer-ear infections by a veterinarian

When a veterinarian first sees a case of otitis externa, he or she will recommend procedures to clean and dry the ear canal. The veterinarian may then prescribe or dispense a medication containing prescription antibiotics that act against several pathogenic organisms at the same time.

The veterinarian may prefer to determine which organisms are causing the infection before starting treatment. This is done by the use of a *culture* and *sensitivity test*. The veterinarian or a technician removes a sample of the exudate from the ear canal and grows the organisms contained in the sample on a special substance called a *culture medium.*

When colonies of the organisms have developed, the veterinarian or the technician will be able to identify the organisms under the microscope. Various medications can be added to the medium to determine which drugs will inhibit the organisms. The veterinarian then can dispense drugs that act against the specific organisms involved in the infection.

Any severe ear infection, any chronic ear infection, and any ear infection that does not improve within a few days may require more treatment than can be accomplished by the use of nonprescription medications. Ear problems that cannot be controlled by keeping the ear canals clean, dry, and of an acid pH should receive professional veterinary attention. Surgery may be necessary in very severe cases.

Hematocyst of the auricle

A *hematocyst* is a large, hot, painful, blood-filled swelling on the inside surface of a dog's ear flap.

The cause of a hematocyst is bleeding between the cartilage and the skin of the ear flap. The bleeding is caused by damage to the ear flap as the patient shakes its head and scratches. Otitis externa or ear mites are found in the ears of many dogs that have hematocysts of the ear flaps. The very rare cases of hematocyst that are not caused by self-inflicted trauma can usually be blamed on dangling metal tags affixed to long-eared dogs' collars; the tags strike the ear flaps when the dogs run.

When a hematocyst first appears, there is active bleeding between the layers of the ear. After twenty-four to forty-eight hours, the bleeding stops and the blood forms a clot. If this condition is not treated, the clotted blood will shrink, drawing the entire ear into a wrinkled mass. The eventual result of an untreated hematocyst is a thickened and deformed ear.

Signs: Sudden appearance. Painful scratching and crying when the ear is touched. The dog holds its head tilted with

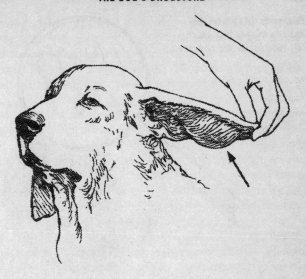

Hematocyst of the auricle.

the affected ear toward the ground. The weight of a hematocyst will cause the upright ear of a dog to tip over or actually hang down.

Treatment: Surgical drainage and appropriate bandaging of a hematocyst must be done under anesthesia. Veterinary attention is necessary to avoid a permanent disfiguration. Important: If the otitis or the mites that caused the hematocyst are not treated, the affected dog will continue to traumatize its ears and often will create another hematocyst.

Ear mites

Often, an owner makes a "diagnosis" of ear mites too quickly when a dog scratches its ears. Bacterial, yeast, and fungal infections are more common causes of canine otitis.

Otodectes cynotis is the ear mite that infects cats, dogs, and a few other animals (but not humans). The mites live

Ear mites. (A) The mites under a magnifying glass. (B) View inside the ear canal.

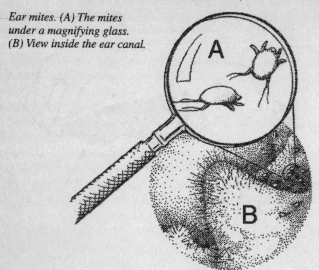

and reproduce in the external ear canal of the host. Ear mites cause intense irritation and itching as they feed by piercing the epidermis and sucking tissue fluids. Thick, dark brown or black wax is produced by the affected ear in response to the irritation caused by the parasite.

Ear mites spread very easily from dog to dog, from dog to cat, and from cat to dog. The mites cannot live away from their hosts. If an adult dog has not been in close contact with dogs or cats of unknown health status, and it has had no source of infection with the mites, then its ear problems are likely to be caused by something else.

Treatment of ear mites will not be successful unless the ears are medicated repeatedly over a course of two or three weeks. The medicine should be applied daily for three days, every other day for three days, then weekly for three weeks. After each treatment except the first, the ear canals should be gently cleaned before new medication is applied. Since mites spread so easily, every animal member of a household, whether or not it has signs of ear mite infection, must be treated.

Signs: Severe scratching of the head and ears. *Otodectes* mites are *almost* large enough to be seen with the naked eye. A person with good eyesight and a bright light source *may* be able to see tiny white specks moving on the surface of a swab of exudate removed from an infected dog's ear. These mites are easily seen if the exudate is examined with an ordinary hand lens or magnifying glass. The mites and their large oval eggs are so common in the ears of infected animals that failure to find them leads to the conclusion that ear mites are not the cause of the patient's problem.

Affected animals: Ear mites are a common parasite in cats and dogs that have received little or no medical attention. A puppy or a kitten purchased from a shelter, from a pet shop, or from a "free to good home" source may come with ear mites. A puppy from a breeder or from a conscientious owner probably will not be affected with ear mites.

Treatment: Ear mites are easy to detect and easy to kill. Eradication of ear mites is accomplished by the following procedures:

• The hard, brown, scaly wax within the ear canal will contain hundreds of mites and their eggs in every stage of development. This wax must be softened and removed. Several treatments with a wax-dissolving medication are necessary to remove all the wax.

• A medication containing an insecticide must be instilled into the ear canal to destroy the remaining mites. Since an insecticide does not destroy the eggs, the medication must be instilled at 4- to 5-day intervals for at least three weeks to destroy new mites as they hatch.

Many OTC dog ear-cleaning products have oil-based formulas that are intended to soften the wax for easier removal. A dropperful of mineral oil or baby oil instilled in the ear will serve the same purpose. "Sweet oil" sold in pharmacies for the softening of wax in human ears is nothing more than purified olive oil. An hour or two after the oil has been instilled, the ear can be cleaned with a cotton swab and the softened wax removed.

A number of nonprescription "ear mite remedies" are on the shelves of every pet store. These preparations usually contain rotenone or pyrethrins, both of which are lethal to ear mites. The insecticide in these products is suspended in an oily substance and will serve the dual purpose of both softening the wax and killing the mites. Success of the treatment depends on the owner's persistence. The medication must be instilled twice a week for three or four weeks after all evidence of mite infestation is gone. If only a few eggs remain to hatch into new mites, the infection will return.

Ear Mite Medications

CHEMICAL	SOME BRAND NAMES
Rotenone	HiLo Earmite Treatment
	MITAPLEX-R
Pyrethrins	NOLVAMITE R-7 EARMITE TREATMENT
	HAPPY JACK MITEX PETMITE

8

SKIN CONDITIONS

Skin problems are among the conditions that are most responsive to treatment with nonprescription drugs. Skin diseases of the dog and the human often are similar in cause, appearance, and treatment. Over-the-counter medications designed for use in human skin conditions are often equally effective in the treatment of skin conditions in the dog.

LET THE USER BEWARE!

Manufacturers of nonprescription medications are not required to prove that their products are effective. The statement *Use only as directed* is the industry disclaimer of responsibility if the product does not perform as expected. Many nonprescription skin preparations that are heavily advertised and in wide use on both humans and dogs contain no ingredients that have been proven to be helpful in the treatment of disease.

Read the label. Using a preparation that contains no effective therapeutic substance is a waste of money, time, and effort.

Certain topical preparations are available in two forms: (1) as a prescription-only drug, and (2) as an OTC drug, usually containing a reduced strength of the same medication. In most cases the therapeutic value of the OTC form will be close to that of the prescription form. In some instances, the OTC form must be applied or administered more frequently.

A CORRECT DIAGNOSIS IS ESSENTIAL FOR SUCCESS

Neither an OTC nor a prescription drug will be helpful if it is used for the wrong condition. Skin diseases are difficult to diagnose. The signs of several different skin conditions may be identical during some stages of the disease process.

The skin has a great ability to heal itself. Many nonparasitic skin conditions need not be treated or need to be treated only with medication designed to make the patient feel better while healing takes place. Except in the case of injuries, skin problems are among the conditions least affected by short delays in starting medication. It is seldom harmful to first try a topical medication, then make an appointment with a veterinarian if the condition does not improve after a few days.

———

It is advisable to seek professional help if the results of topical OTC medications are not as expected after five to seven days.

———

THE PROCESS OF SKIN HEALING

A *laceration* is a cut or incision. A *superficial laceration* is a cut that does not penetrate through all the layers of the skin. A *deep laceration* is a cut that penetrates into the underlying muscle or other tissue. An *abrasion* is a scrape or wound that injures only the surface of the skin. A *contusion* is a bruise: tissue damage caused by blunt trauma. Damage to skin and underlying tissue may be mild, such as in a scald, or severe, such as in a burn.

Granulomas and *calluses* are growths that develop on the skin in response to continuous irritation. Thickenings of this type are the body's attempt to protect the site of the irritation.

As skin heals, new cells grow to bridge the defect. *Healing by first intention* takes place only when the edges of a clean wound are held together in perfect alignment. Healing by first intention does not take place except in the case of sterile surgical incisions or debrided and sutured lesions in which no dead tissue or bacteria remain.

Lacerations, abrasions, and contusions all heal by *second intention*. *Nonviable* (dead) tissue sloughs away and new cells grow to fill the gap. When the gap is filled, healing is complete. The presence of visible scar tissue depends on the extent of the injury and the regenerative powers of each type of tissue.

If an injury is contaminated with dirt and bacteria, the body's defenses prevent healing from taking place. *Leukocytes* (white blood cells) rush into the damaged area and attempt to engulf the foreign substances. These leukocytes form pus, which contains debris, bacteria, and dead cells. Pus removes these contaminants by flowing out of the wound. A scab of dried fluid may form over the surface of the injury, but if debris and infection remain under the scab, pus will continue to form and healing will not take place.

FORMS OF MEDICATIONS FOR THE SKIN

Medications intended for application to the skin consist of one or more *active ingredients* dissolved or suspended in a *vehicle*. Many preparations also contain one or more *inert ingredients* such as preservatives or fragrances. The form in which the medication is supplied depends on the vehicle in which the active ingredients are presented.

• *Ointments* have as a vehicle a thick substance that is insoluble in water, such as white petroleum jelly. These products are intended to keep the active ingredients in contact with the affected areas while acting as barriers to the evaporation of moisture.

• *Cremes, vanishing cremes, and lotions* consist of active ingredients suspended in thick, water-soluble vehicles.

When absorbed, these products carry the active ingredients into the superficial layers of the skin.

• *Liquids* consist of drugs dissolved in a fluid vehicle such as water, alcohol, or propylene glycol.

• *Medicated Shampoos* contain the usual detergent and fragrance components of ordinary shampoos together with one or more active ingredients designed to treat specific medical problems of the skin. *Keratolytic and antiseborrheic agents* loosen, dissolve, or remove scales or excess oil from the skin. Many human and veterinary shampoos are very similar; the human products are often more easily obtained and less expensive than are the veterinary products.

• *Sprays* are liquids supplied in a pressurized container. The purpose of sprays is to allow the medication to be applied to the area without touching the lesion.

• *Scrubs* and *skin cleansers* are liquids that include a soap or detergent agent. These products aid in removing surface contamination of an affected area.

• *Powders* and *powder-sprays* are drugs in a dry vehicle such as talc or boric acid powder. Powders are usually supplied in "shaker" or "puffer" containers, powder-sprays in a pressurized container.

The treatment of a dog's skin is complicated by the presence of hair. In many cases, the hair must be removed if the area is to be treated properly. See page 43 for detailed instructions on hair removal and application of topical medications.

CLASSIFICATION OF MEDICATIONS FOR THE SKIN

• *Antibiotics* are substances that are antagonistic to the growth of specific bacteria.

• *Antimicrobial drugs* includes chemicals that destroy bacteria by physical means, such as by destroying the cell walls of the organisms. *Antibiotics* are specific types of antimicrobial drugs.

• *Anti-inflammatory agents* act on cellular response to noxious agents. The purpose of topical anti-inflammatory drugs is to reduce pain, itching, and swelling of damaged tissue.

• *Antiseborrheic agents* help to remove surface skin oils and dead cells.

THE USE OF OTC MEDICATIONS FOR SKIN PROBLEMS

Many medications that are designed to be used on the skin are useful to treat several conditions. For example, *nitrofurazone* ointment, powders, and sprays are useful to control wound infections and also to treat other skin problems such as local *pyoderma,* or pus-filled lesions. *Bacitracin* antibiotic ointment may be used on surface wounds as well as on infected calluses.

The majority of nonprescription, OTC topical medications are intended for human use. Most of these products can be used as well on the canine patient.

All medical students learn this principle of wound treatment: a moist wound is best treated with a dry medication, a dry wound with a moist one. A powder, a creme, or a spray is used, therefore, on weeping or damp lesions; an ointment is used on dry, scabby lesions.

Almost all topical medications can be applied as often as

needed. A few preparations have a limit of two to four applications in every twenty-four-hour period.

Most preparations can be applied under bandages. The instructions on the label state which medications should not. In a few instances, the medication should be allowed to dry before a bandage is applied. No bandage on a dog (or on a human) should be left in place without changing for more than twenty-four hours. If bandages on dogs' feet get wet or torn, they must be replaced at once.

Dogs are likely to lick the areas to which medication is applied. Not only does licking remove the medication from the affected area, but some topical drugs can be harmful if taken internally. See page 48 for ways to combat this problem.

It is not advisable to apply topical anesthetic (pain-relieving) agents to areas that a dog can lick. If licked, the anesthetic agents will cause the dog to have a temporarily numb tongue. The dog will paw at its mouth or otherwise act disturbed by the sensation.

SKIN CONDITIONS CAUSED BY INJURY OR INFECTION

—

If you or your child had this condition, would you treat it yourself or rush to a hospital emergency room?

—

Minor cuts, scrapes, nicks, and bumps on a child or an adult human are treated with medication applied to the area and maybe the application of a Band-Aid. Deep lacerations and extensive abrasions warrant a trip to the doctor. Minor damage to the skin of dogs can be handled exactly as it is with humans, with three exceptions.

1. Dogs in pain may bite. Dogs cannot understand that a procedure that causes pain may be in their best interest. Dogs' instincts cause them to try to avoid further injury by

resisting examination and treatment of their wounds. See page 44 for instructions on restraining an injured dog.

2. Dogs instinctively lick their wounds to remove contaminants and dead tissue. In the process of licking, dogs also remove medications that are applied to their wounds. In order to be effective in a dog's wound, medication must penetrate the tissues before the dog has a chance to lick it away. See page 48 for ways to prevent the dog from licking medication.

3. Dogs hate bandages. Dogs dislike anything irritating applied or attached to their skin, and will attempt to chew off or scratch off gauze, tape, and even sutures.

Should you apply bandages?

Bandages serve many functions. Bandages cover a wound to prevent contamination, they cushion a wound to prevent pain, they keep medications in contact with a wound, they prevent exudate from a wound from soiling the environment, they exclude air from a wound, and a bandaged wound is not as unattractive as an open one.

Bandaging a dog's foot

Dogs' feet are a common site of wounds and dermatitis. It seems reasonable that a protective bandage would help injuries on dogs' feet. This is usually the complete opposite of the truth. Suppose a person with a wound on his heel had a tape-and-gauze bandage applied over his entire foot. Suppose this person walked, indoors and out, on the bandage without covering the tape with anything more substantial than a plastic bag. Suppose the bandage was allowed to remain unchanged on this person's foot for several days. What would happen?

Moisture from the environment would seep through the

tape and dampen the gauze. Sweat from the patient's foot would create even more moisture within the bandage. The patient's body heat would keep the area nice and warm. Exudate such as blood and serum would be held inside the wound. Pathogenic microorganisms such as bacteria and fungi would flourish. Imagine what the wound would look like and smell like when the bandage was finally removed.

The same conditions exist inside the bandage on a dog's foot. The obvious conclusion is that dogs' feet should not be bandaged unless it is absolutely necessary. Bandages that are applied to dogs' feet must be removed and changed a minimum of every twelve hours. It is extremely important that any bandage that is intended to remain on the foot for more than two or three hours must not be applied tightly enough to cut off the circulation.

One injury of a dog's foot does require a tight bandage: a deep laceration of a footpad that is accompanied by copious bleeding. Dogs can hardly bleed to death from a cut footpad, but they can lose a significant amount of blood. A pressure bandage applied to stop bleeding must be removed within three hours. If the circulation to a dog's foot is compromised

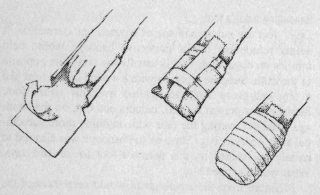

Bandaging the paw.

for a longer period, the tissues that are without adequate blood supply may die. Gangrene may be the result.

For information on applying other types of bandages, see p. 52.

Applying a pressure bandage to stop bleeding

- The wound is covered with several layers of sterile gauze pads; cotton is placed between the toes to prevent the formation of pressure sores.
- A tape strip is applied to extend below the foot. This will be incorporated within the tape to keep the dog from shaking off the bandage.
- The foot is wrapped in three or four layers of gauze.
- Tape is applied over the gauze in two directions, incorporating the first strip. The tape is applied snugly to exert pressure over the wound.

This plastic collar prevents the dog from disturbing its injuries.

Preventing dogs from disturbing their injuries

A variety of devices are intended to prevent dogs from licking or otherwise disturbing their injuries. The collar illustrated here makes it impossible (or at least extremely difficult) for the wearer to reach its lesion with its mouth. This collar can be homemade with a piece of thin, stiff material such as cardboard or with a plastic bucket of appropriate size. The collar is not comfortable for the wearer and should be reserved for use in extreme cases. Products intended to prevent chewing and licking by making bandages and wounds unpalatable are not reliable; a dog may decide to tolerate a bitter or peppery flavor in order to chew its bandage or lick its wound.

Treat minor wounds correctly

- Stop the bleeding. If bleeding is extensive, a trip to a veterinarian is indicated.
- Clean the wound with mild soap or a medicated cleanser; flush the wound free of debris with large amounts of clean water.
- Blot the wound dry with clean towels.
- Apply medication to control infection.
- Keep area clean and reapply the medication as needed.

Hundreds of OTC medications are sold for application to wounds and abrasions. Each of these products contains one or more ingredients intended to inhibit the growth of bacteria, and to lubricate, dry, or protect the surface of the wound. In the majority of cases, nonprescription wound products are adequate for the treatment of superficial lesions on both man and dog.

Pyoderma

The term *pyoderma* means "pus in the skin." *Generalized pyoderma* occurs when a large part of the patient's body is affected. This condition is often secondary to conditions that cause suppression of dogs' immune systems. *Local pyoderma* occurs when only specific areas of the skin are involved.

Antimicrobial skin cleansers: For Use in Wound Cleansing

ACTIVE INGREDIENT	SOME BRAND NAMES (all reduce microorganisms)
Benzethonium chloride	CLINICAL CARE ANTIMICROBIAL WOUND CLEANSER
Chloroxylenol	CONCEPT ANTIMICROBIAL DERMAL CLEANSER
Providone-iodine	BETADINE SKIN CLEANSER

Antimicrobial Medications To Control Wound Infection

CHEMICAL NAME	SOME BRAND NAMES	HOW SUPPLIED
Iodine compounds	IOSPRAY	liquid spray
Providone-iodine	BETADINE OINTMENT	ointment
	FURACIN DRESSING	ointment
Nitrofurazone	NITROFURACIN	ointment
	FURA-DRESSING	

Signs: The lesions of pyoderma are moist and painful areas of pus and scabs.

• *Lip-fold pyoderma* is often called "cocker mouth" because the breeds affected with this condition are those with deep lip folds.

• *Vulvar-fold pyoderma* occurs around the vulva of obese older females.

• *Nasal-fold pyoderma* occurs in the nasal folds of short-faced breeds such as the Pekingese.

• *Interdigital pyoderma,* sometimes called "winter paws," occurs between the toes and between the footpads of any breed; this condition is most common during wet, cold weather.

Cause: Pyoderma is an infection caused by the growth of microorganisms in natural folds of dogs' skin. The microorganisms involved usually are *Streptococcus* or *Staphylococcus* bacteria.

Signs: Brown staining of the skin and hair of the affected areas is a constant finding in cases of local pyoderma. Pain, scabs, and odor are also characteristics of generalized and local pyodermas. Dogs with lip-fold pyoderma or nasal-fold pyoderma appear to have extreme halitosis. The entire body of a female with vulvar-fold pyoderma is odoriferous. Interdigital pyodermas smell the least; dogs lick these lesions and keep them relatively free of debris.

Treatment: *Generalized pyoderma* is treated successfully only by a prolonged course of oral and topical prescription antibiotics. Only a veterinarian should treat a dog suspected of having generalized pyoderma.

Local pyoderma: The organisms that cause pyoderma flourish in the folds of dogs' skin because these areas are constantly moist and warm. Treatment of the condition is directed to keeping the areas dry, thus eliminating the conditions favorable to bacterial growth.

In a few cases, relief of local pyoderma can only be accomplished if the folds of skin are removed by surgery. In most cases, the treatment is simpler.

The least difficult way to treat local pyoderma is to remove the hair with an electric clipper and a surgical shaving blade, followed by the application of an **antiseptic** or **an-**

tibiotic powder every twelve hours until the condition is
under control. If a clipper is not available, the hair can be
carefully removed with curved scissors. Since the hair must
be removed at approximately two-week intervals, owners of
dogs with recurrent local pyoderma will find that the purchase of a clipper is a good investment.

Medications to Treat Local Pyoderma
(After Hair Is Removed from the Affected Areas)

CHEMICAL NAME	SOME BRAND NAMES	HOW SUPPLIED
Bacitracin	BACITRACIN Topical Ointment	ointment
Polymicin and bacitracin	POLYSPORIN	powder
Benzethonium chloride	FORMULA MAGIC	powder
Iodine compounds	BETADINE AEROSOL	spray
Nitrofurazone	FURACIN Soluble Powder	powder
Oxytetracycline with hydrocortisone	TERRA-CORTRIL SPRAY	spray

Application of these agents only once every three or four
days will prevent local pyoderma from coming back *as long
as the hair is removed regularly*. If the hair is allowed to
grow, the condition will surely return.

SKIN PROBLEMS CAUSED BY OTHER FACTORS

Injury and infection are not the only cause of nonparasitic
skin disease of the dog. Just as can humans, dogs can suffer
from skin problems caused by noxious agents to which they
are sensitive. Many dogs suffer from abnormal skin condi-

tions that are inherited or from conditions that accompany large size or old age. Nonprescription medications have many applications to these conditions. In some of these cases, the routine application of nonprescriptions is the treatment of choice to control the problem.

Allergic dermatitis

This condition may be generalized (all over the dog) or localized (only in one or two places.)

Cause: The saliva of fleas is by far the most common allergen that causes generalized dermatitis in dogs. Other causes are sensitivity to certain food such as wheat or beef, and allergy to airborne substances such as grass pollen.

Signs: Generalized allergic dermatitis is manifest by extremely itchy skin. The patient chews and scratches incessantly until it has damaged the skin over its rump and sides. Self-inflicted skin damage is often severe enough to cause hair loss and moist, bleeding areas.

Treatment: The treatment of allergic dermatitis is based on removing the cause. Since fleas are the most common cause of this condition, the first step in relieving the signs of allergic dermatitis is to destroy fleas. Even if no fleas can be found, they may still be the cause of allergic dermatitis. Many dogs are so allergic to the saliva of fleas that only a few fleabites will cause the dogs to have an intense reaction.

The few cases of allergic dermatitis that are not caused by fleas are difficult to diagnose and treat. These cases will require the assistance of a veterinary dermatologist.

Medication: For flea control, see Chapter 9.

Nonprescription antihistamines are among the most popular medications used to alleviate human symptoms of upper respiratory conditions such as colds, flu, and seasonal allergies. Antihistamine preparations are formulated to reduce human allergic response. Even though dogs do not catch human colds or flu, some of these preparations have use in controlling allergic responses of dogs.

Nonprescritpion Anti-inflammatory Preparations For Use in Allergic-Dermatitis

CHEMICAL NAME	SOME BRAND NAMES	HOW SUPPLIED
Oxytetracycline with hydrocortisone	TERRA-CORTRIL SPRAY	spray
Hydrocortisone	CORTAID	cream, ointment
	NUPERCAINAL ANTI-ITCH	cream

Many generics are available.

Oral and Topical Antihistamines That May Be Useful for Allergic Dogs

DRUG	SOME BRAND NAMES	DOSE
Chlorphenerimine maleata	CHLOR-TRIMETON	2 to 8 mg every 8 hrs. (1 or 2 tablets)
Clemastine fumerate	TAVIST-D	1 mg per dog, every 12 hrs. (1 tablet)
Diphenhydramine HCl	BENADRYL ALLERGY	25 to 50 mg every 8 hrs. (1 or 2 tablets or caplets)

**Oral and Topical Antihistamines
That May Be Useful for Allergic Dogs (*continued*)**

DRUG	SOME BRAND NAMES	DOSE
	BENADRYL ITCH STOPPING CREAM OR STICK	may be useful on hot spots, or moist dermatitis

Comments: Discontinue treatment when signs subside. All of the above drugs are available in many other brands and as generics.

Antihistamines are often combined with analgesics and decongestants in one preparation to treat several human symptoms at the same time. Since the canine response to drugs is not always the same as the human response, only human preparations that consist of a single active ingredient are recommended for dogs.

Callus
This is the formation of thickened layers of hyperkeratotic skin at the pressure points on a dog's body. Pressure points are the sites where the skin covers bony prominence, such as the elbows, the outer surfaces of the hocks, and the points of the hips.

Cause: Constant pressure of the bones against the skin when the dog lies down. Almost every large dog over three or four years of age has calluses on its elbows and on its hocks. Calluses can become infected with bacteria and form large, nonhealing sores.

To aid in the prevention of calluses, the area of the callus must be kept soft and lubricated, and the dog must be kept from lying on hard surfaces. A bed made of an orthopedic foam mattress pad covered with carpeting is recommended.

Commercial products such as water beds for dogs are available.

Medications to Prevent and Treat Calluses

CHEMICAL NAME	SOME BRAND NAMES	HOW SUPPLIED
Bacitracin	BACITRACIN Topical Ointment	ointment
Bacitracin and Polymicin	POLYSPORIN	ointment
Chlorhexidine	NOLVASAN OINTMENT	ointment
Petroleum jelly	VASELINE Many generics available	
Triple antibiotic	Many generics are available	ointment

Contact dermatitis

This condition is uncommon on dogs.

Cause: Contact to the skin of a toxic material.

Signs: The lesions appear as a rash on the sites of contact with the offending substances, most often on the affected dogs' belly or feet.

Treatment: Consists of washing off the allergen and applying **anti-inflammatory cremes, ointments,** or **sprays.** The same agents are used to treat "hot spots," or moist dermatitis. See page 98.

Dandruff

Signs: The appearance of flakes of dead skin in the coat. Dandruff is most obvious as flakes of loose skin on short-haired dogs and on dogs with genetically thin hair coats.

Cause: Normal sloughing of cells from the outer layer of the skin. As skin cells grow, the old cells slough off. It is only when sloughing is very excessive that the condition is considered to be dandruff.

Dandruff on a dog is seldom caused by lack of fatty acids or anything else missing in the dog's diet, no more than such factors cause human dandruff. Modern dogs fed modern dogfood, at least the better brands of dogfood, rarely suffer from skin problems caused by the lack of essential nutrients. The inclusion of supplements in a dog's diet probably will not eliminate its dandruff. Giving supplements *plus* brushing and bathing the dog in appropriate keratolytic shampoo probably will resolve the problem.

Treatment: Most dogs with dandruff need only a good brushing and bathing.

Medication: Many **human dandruff shampoos** contain the same ingredients as do **canine dandruff shampoos.** The majority of these products can be used interchangeably by both humans and dogs. These shampoos are also used to treat *canine seborrheic dermatitis.* See chart of shampoos on page 102.

Eczema
This is not a specific disease. *Eczema* is a general term for inflammatory skin conditions. A better term for eczema is *moist dermatitis*.

"Hot spots" (moist dermatitis)
Signs: Local areas of moist dermatitis that occur on dogs' rumps or sides of their heads. These lesions seem to appear suddenly. They are called "hot spots" because they resemble thermal burns.

Cause: Hot spots are local manifestations of a generalized allergic condition, most often fleabite allergy.

Medications Used to Treat "Hot Spots"

CHEMICAL NAME	SOME BRAND NAMES	HOW SUPPLIED
Iodine compounds	IOSPRAY	spray
Nitrofurazone	FURACIN SOLUBLE POWDER	powder
	Many generics are available	powder
Oxytetracycline with hydrocortisone	TERRA-CORTRIL SPRAY	spray
Polymicin and bacitracin	POLYSPORIN	powder
Povidone iodine	BETADINE AEROSOL	spray

Treatment: Elimination of the cause (usually fleas) and local application of **anitmicrobial** and **anti-inflammatory agents.**

Lick granuloma

Signs: This condition is common in certain large, short-haired breeds of dogs such as the Doberman pinscher and the Labrador retriever. The affected dog licks an area, usually on the carpus (wrist), until it has created a raw spot.

Cause: The cause of lick granuloma is unknown. Some authorities attribute lick granuloma to boredom—the dog has nothing to do, so it licks its foot. It has even been suggested that the dog that has a lick granuloma be given a companion of the same species to occupy its attention.

A more logical theory of the cause of lick granuloma is that the skin in the area is irritated by frequent contact with the ground when the dog lies down, much the same as the cause of callus formation. The carpal area is a much more convenient site for a dog to lick than is the elbow.

Lick granuloma is self-perpetuating: The more the dog licks, the more the lesion itches; the more it itches, the more the dog licks. Eventually the dog has a permanently damaged area on its foot.

Whether the cause is physical or psychological, dogs that have had major changes in their environments have been known to stop licking their wrists and to allow the lesions to heal.

Treatment: Successful treatment of lick granuloma is extremely difficult. Unless tranquilized or restrained, dogs invariably lick off medication and tear off bandages applied to the area. Even surgical removal of these lesions is often unsuccessful, since the affected area has little loose skin that can be closed over an incision. Veterinarians have tried to treat lick granuloma with intralesional injection of corticosteroids, with varying success.

Medication: Frequent application of **topical anesthetics** intended to be used on sunburn on humans has been useful in some cases. **Anti-inflammatory** and **antibiotic wound sprays and powders** will help if the dog is prevented from licking them away before the medication has a chance to act in the area.

Nonprescription Topical Anesthetic Agents that May Be Useful for the Treatment of Lick Granuloma

ACTIVE INGREDIENTS	SOME BRAND NAMES	HOW SUPPLIED
Lidocaine	BACTINE ANTISEPTIC	liquid & pump spray
Benzalkonium chloride	ANESTHETIC LIQUID	
Benzocaine	AMERICAINE TOPICAL ANESTHETIC	aerosol spray & ointment

Nonprescription Topical Anesthetic Agents that May Be Useful for the Treatment of Lick Granuloma (*continued*)

ACTIVE INGREDIENTS	SOME BRAND NAMES	HOW SUPPLIED
	SOLARCAINE MEDICATED FIRST AID	aerosol spray
Dibucaine	NUPERCAINAL OINTMENT	ointment
Lidocaine	XYLOCAINE 2.5% OINTMENT	ointment
Pramoxine HCl with Polymicin and Neomycin	NEOSPORIN PLUS	cream

Dose: Apply as often as needed.

Seborrhea

This is "greasy skin disease." Seborrhea is known to be hereditary in certain breeds of dogs such as the American cocker spaniel. Affected dogs are born with the trait, although the condition may not become apparent until the dog is more than a year old.

Signs: Greasy skin, itching, scratching, and a bad odor from the skin. The irritation and odor are caused by secondary bacterial growth in the sebum (the oily secretion of skin glands).

Cause: An excessive production and discharge of sebum.

Treatment: Seborrhea can be controlled but not cured. Treatment consists of regular bathing with **medicated shampoos.** Most dogs with this condition can be maintained as acceptable pets with a good scrubbing every week or two. Human and animal **anitseborrhea shampoos** are available OTC; either can be used on both species with equally good results.

Medicated Shampoos
For use in Dandruff and Seborrhea

ACTIVE INGREDIENT	SOME BRAND NAMES	ACTION
Chlorhexidine	NOLVASAN SHAMPOO	antimicrobial
Chloroxylenol	CONCEPT ANTI-MICROBIAL SHAMPOO	antimicrobial (infant and geriatic)
	MG 217 SHAMPOO	antiseborrheic
	TEGRIN DANDRUFF SHAMPOO	antiseborrheic
Coal tar	NEUTROGENA T/GEL SHAMPOO	antiseborrheic
	DENOREX MEDICATED SHAMPOO	antiseborrheic
	SULFUR TAR SHAMPOO (vet)	antiseborrheic
Coal tar, sulfur, & salicylic acid	SEBTAR SHAMPOO (vet)	antiseborrheic
Iodine compound	WELLADOL SHAMPOO (vet)	antibacterial
Pyrithione zinc	HEAD & SHOULDERS DANDRUFF SHAMPOO	keratolytic
	X-SEB SHAMPOO	keratolytic
Selenium sulfide	HEAD & SHOULDERS INTENSIVE TREATMENT SHAMPOO	antiseborrheic
	SELEEN SHAMPOO (vet)	antiseborrheic
	SELSUN BLUE DANDRUFF SHAMPOO	antiseborrheic
Sulfur	THIONIUM SHAMPOO	antiseborrheic
	MICODEX TAR & SULFUR PET SHAMPOO (vet)	

Urticaria ("hives")

Signs: A dog with an allergic reaction may appear to have lumps on its skin, a roughened hair coat, a swollen nose, and difficulty breathing. Dogs with allergic reactions often scratch just as do humans with hives.

Cause: Unusual protein, such as the venom of a bee sting. A few dogs have allergic reactions to vaccinations.

Treatment: Unless the patient is experiencing difficulty in breathing, no treatment is needed for allergic reactions as most of these conditions go away within a few hours. If a dog with hives seems to have respiratory difficulty, the condition should be treated as an emergency and the patient taken to the nearest veterinary hospital without delay.

Medication: Usually none needed. Human oral antihistamines are of little value in treating allergic reactions in dogs. Veterinarians usually treat hives with an injection of a steroid.

Tumors of the skin

Tumors may be benign or malignant. Malignant tumors should be excised as soon as they are detected. Any growth in a dog's mouth or any unexplained mass that ulcerates, bleeds, or grows quickly, should be seen by a veterinarian.

Mammary tumors (breast cancer) are the most common tumor of the canine species. Mammary tumors occur in unspayed females or in females spayed after they have experienced several heat periods. Early-stage mammary tumors feel like hard, lumpy areas in the mammary glands. Mammary tumors should be surgically removed as soon as they are detected. Dogs can be protected from mammary tumor development by early spaying. Mammary tumors are almost unknown on dogs spayed before puberty.

Perianal adenomas (tumors around the anus) occur primarily on unneutered male dogs. Just as with mammary tumors, neutering is both preventive and therapeutic.

Diagnosis and treatment of skin tumors on dogs are similar to the methods used for humans. With prompt attention, most skin tumors are not life threatening.

Two types of benign tumors can safely be ignored unless they occur in a position that is harmful to the dog. These are papillomas and lipomas.

A *papilloma* is a benign tumor of the outer layers of the skin. These are common on older short-haired dogs, but can occur on older dogs with every type of coat. Papillomas are raised, warty growths about the size of a pea. The surface of a papilloma is lumpy and often covered with greasy discharge from the skin glands. Occasionally the surface becomes damaged and bleeds. Individual papillomas do not grow significantly larger, but dogs affected with this condition usually develop many more growths over the surface of their bodies. Papillomas may occur on the dog's neck and head; they are rare on the limbs.

Surgical removal of papillomas is for cosmetic reasons only. Removing existing papillomas will not prevent the development of others.

Lipomas are fat-filled cysts under the skin. These growths are not attached to the underlying tissue. Lipomas are soft, smooth masses that never feel solid or lumpy. Lipomas often grow in size. Occasionally they rupture and discharge their contents.

To confirm the diagnosis of a lipoma, a veterinarian performs a test called an *aspiration biopsy.* The veterinarian inserts a hypodermic needle into the mass and withdraws a tiny portion of the contents of the cyst. The material is then placed on a slide and examined under a microscope. Lipomas are usually harmless to the dog, but large lipomas may require removal by a veterinarian.

Treatment of skin tumors always requires professional management. Surgery, laser ablation, cryosurgery, and radiation are among the options available for dogs' tumors, just as they are for humans' tumors.

9

FLEAS AND FLEA CONTROL

Fleas are *ectoparasites*. These are creatures that spend all or part of their life cycle on the skin of another animal. The animal that harbors an ectoparasite is the *host*. Some ectoparasites never leave their host's body; some move from host to host; some must live on or in hosts of several different species in order to complete their life cycles. Fleas are ectoparasites that spend only their adult lives on the host. The eggs, larvae, and cocoons of the flea develop in the hosts' environment.

Fleas cause a large percentage of all dogs' skin disease. Fleas pierce the epidermis of the dog and suck blood from the small capillaries in the dog's skin. During the process of feeding, the flea injects its saliva into the outer layers of the dog's skin. This saliva prevents the blood from clotting so that the flea can feed.

The saliva of the flea is a powerful antigen that produces an allergic response in the dog that is bitten. This allergic response causes pruritus (severe itching) of the infested dog's skin. Lesions on the skin are not caused by the fleas but by the damage done by the dog itself as it bites and scratches skin in an attempt to relieve the itching.

The severity of the dog's response depends on the allergic sensitivity of the dog more than on the number of fleas that the dog harbors. Some dogs can be heavily infested with fleas and have little reaction; some dogs receive only a fleabite or two and scratch themselves raw for days or weeks. Sensitivity to flea saliva appears to increase with exposure. Young dogs are less reactive to the antigen than are older dogs.

Dogs that are extremely sensitive to fleabites often damage themselves to the extent that the skin of their lower backs and thighs is permanently thickened, wrinkled, and hairless. If the traumatized areas become infected with microorganisms, the animal will develop areas that have scabs, crusts, and a fetid odor. A dog with severe allergic flea dermatitis is a miserable sight, and the owner of such a dog is unhappy watching his pet constantly scratch and chew its skin.

DIAGNOSIS OF FLEABITE ALLERGY

The presence of fleas, of course, is a positive diagnosis. Very few dogs that have fleas will not have an allergic response. Most dog owners can recognize fleas: dark-colored insects less than an eighth inch in length that run through the dog's hair. Fleas can be found most frequently on the dog's lower belly and the dog's back in front of its tail. The feces of fleas appear on infested dogs as dark brown grainy particles in the coat. Flea feces consists largely of partially digested blood. If these particles are dissolved in water, the red color of hemoglobin will appear. When a dog with a heavy flea infestation is bathed, the water will be stained red by dissolved flea feces.

The apparent absence of fleas does not rule out a diagnosis of fleabite allergy. A few dogs' pruritus may be caused by an allergic response to an inhalant such as house dust or grass pollen, or even to a sensitivity to some ingredient in its diet. However, these conditions are so much less common than fleabite allergy that every scratching dog should be treated for fleas before it undergoes extensive testing for other allergies. It does not take many fleas to cause a sensitive dog to have a reaction. The dog that apparently is free of fleas may have such a small infestation that the fleas go unnoticed.

Fleabite allergy is so common that a type of involuntary action by infested dogs has been called the "flea" or "scratch" reflex. A positive flea reflex is shown when a dog is rubbed along one side of its spine, and the hind leg on the same side makes involuntary scratching motions.

THE LIFE CYCLE OF THE FLEA

Fleas are members of the class *Insecta,* the insects. *Pulex irritans* is the human flea. In some parts of the world this parasite still causes dermatitis in the human population. *Ctenocephalides canis* and *C. felis* are the common dog and cat fleas. Unfortunately, though, fleas are not very host-specific; a flea is perfectly happy to thrive on more than one species of hosts. For example, the cat flea is the most common parasite of dogs as well as of cats. Dog and cat fleas will bite humans (and cause pruritic welts) but cannot complete their life cycle on the human species.

An understanding of the life cycle of the flea is necessary to control the flea population.

• Adult fleas feed, mate, and lay eggs on their hosts. The eggs of the flea are white, oval, and almost microscopic in size. A female flea will produce several hundred eggs in her lifetime. The female flea lays eggs on the host, but the eggs do not adhere to the host's hair.

• The eggs of the flea fall off the host into the host's bedding, carpeting, cracks between floorboards, or wherever the flea-infested dog rests. The eggs hatch in a few days to a few weeks, depending on the temperature and humidity of the environment.

• Flea larvae that emerge from the eggs resemble tiny, hairy worms. These larvae feed on organic matter, including scales from dogs' skin, hair, fibers of wool carpeting, tape-

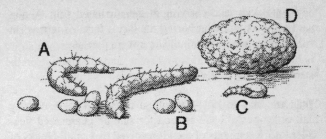

Stages in flea development: (A) larva; (B) eggs; (C) larva hatching from egg; (D) cocoon from which an adult flea will emerge.

worm segments, and the excrement of adult fleas. Larvae shed their skins twice as they grow.

• When they are fully developed, flea larvae form cocoons. Adult fleas emerge from the cocoons in two to four weeks, again depending on the temperature and humidity of the environment. The newly emerged fleas seek a host upon which to feed, mate, and continue the life cycle.

Only the adult fleas live on the bodies of their hosts. The eggs, larvae, and pupae develop in the host's environment.

FLEAS CAUSE MORE THAN ITCHING

In addition to the irritation they cause dogs, fleas are vectors of at least two diseases that affect humans: bubonic plague and typhus. In parts of the United States, notably the Southwest, flea-infested dogs can be carriers of serious human illness.

Fleas are also the intermediate host of the common dog tapeworm. Flea larvae feed upon tapeworm segments that are passed by the dog. When these larvae become adult fleas, they carry the immature form of the tapeworm within their bodies. Dogs often swallow fleas by accident while they are licking and chewing at their irritated skin. A dog that swallows a flea harboring the larval form of tapeworm will become infected with the tapeworm parasite.

METHODS OF FLEA CONTROL

Fleas are easy to kill—individual fleas, that is. A novelty mail-order house once offered for sale a "guaranteed flea-killer kit." Recipients of the kit received two small blocks of wood, one marked "A," the other marked "B." The instructions with the kit read: "Place flea on block A. Press firmly with block B."

Until a few years ago, flea control was only a little more sophisticated than the novelty flea-killer kit. Medications for the purpose had to be toxic enough to kill fleas but safe enough to apply to dogs and cats. The active ingredient of most flea powders and sprays was *pyrethrin,* a natural plant extract that effectively kills those fleas with which it comes in contact, but has little residual action and thus must be applied very frequently. Flea eradication that is directed only toward killing the adult fleas is a slow method of reducing the flea population.

Recent advances in flea control have made old-fashioned short-acting powders and sprays obsolete. Products are available that kill fleas in several stages of their life cycles and which continue their action for weeks or even months. Pyrethrins are still in use, often in combination with other drugs, but synthetic insecticides now dominate the market.

Modern flea-eradication preparations are of two types. One type consists of insecticides that are absorbed into the skin of the host and act for prolonged periods to kill adult fleas that feed on the host. These types of products are available as whole-body dips, sprays, and "one spot" applications to be applied to a single area of the host's skin.

The other type of flea-eradication product is a tablet or liquid that is administered monthly to the host. Fleas that feed upon treated hosts produce only eggs that do not hatch, thus breaking the flea's life cycle. If a drug of this type is used, results will be seen much more quickly if it is used in conjunction with a medication that kills adult fleas. At this time, the oral product is available in the United States only by veterinary prescription.

Some of the drugs that are designed for topical application are available only by prescription. Some are sold OTC in every pet and feed store. Are prescription drugs safer? Are they more effective? Both prescription and nonprescription flea killers contain similar types of long-lasting synthetic insecticides and insect growth regulators. Both will eradicate fleas safely if used according to directions. Whichever product is chosen, dogs need no longer suffer from uncontrolled dermatitis and pruritus caused by these parasites.

Various herbal drugs such as citrus oil are sold for flea control. Also available are electronic "flea repellers" and "flea traps" that consist of a low-watt lightbulb in a reflector suspended over a pan of water. Owners who rely on these methods of flea destruction are better advised to purchase the two little blocks of wood.

Original "flea powders" had limited action

Modern parasite-control products are remarkably effective compared to those of only a few years ago. Original "flea powders" contained either pyrethrins or rotenone, which are organic insecticides derived from plants. These products kill only those fleas with which the powder comes into direct contact. Adult fleas that escape the application of the powder live to bite and produce another population of parasites.

Although products of this type are extremely nontoxic to dogs and cats, the chemicals have little or no lasting action. Within forty-eight hours, a dog treated with pyrethrins or rotenone can be infested with new fleas. Dogs living in heavily flea-infested environments must be treated with rotenone or pyrethrin powders, dips, or sprays at least every other day if the drugs are to reduce the dog's flea burden.

Flea eggs and pupae in the environment are not affected when insecticides such as pyrethrins or rotenone are applied to the host. The life cycle of the flea continues even though some of the adults are destroyed.

Preparations containing pyrethrins and rotenone are still widely used to control dogs' fleas. These drugs are safe to use on puppies and kittens. They are inexpensive. Permethrin, a synthetic pyrethrin, has a significantly longer length of action than the naturally derived chemical.

New drugs control fleas more effectively

There are, however, newer drugs that control ectoparasites both on and off the host more thoroughly and with less effort on the part of the owner. With the use of these drugs, no dog needs to suffer from the constant irritation of fleabite allergy.

• *Do these products work better than the old ones?* Yes, they certainly do. Preparations are available that will eliminate fleas and ticks for months at a time. Many of these products attack the parasites at more than one stage of the life cycle.

• *Are these products safe for use on dogs?* Yes, *only* if used according to directions. Misuse of the newer drugs can have serious consequences.

• *Are the newer products easier to use?* Ask anyone who has dusted powder all over a dog every two days if he would rather give the dog a tablet, or apply the contents of a small tube of liquid to the dog's skin once a month. The newer products have revolutionized the flea-control industry.

• *Are these products harmful to the environment?* Not unless they are misused or the containers are disposed of improperly.

—

Many pesticides that are safe for dogs are deadly to cats. Never use dog products on cats in any amounts unless the label specifies "for dogs and cats."

—

TYPES OF CHEMICALS FOR ECTOPARASITE CONTROL

- *Insecticides* kill adult insect parasites with which the drug comes into direct contact. Examples are pyrethrins and rotenone, which are derived from plants.
- *Insecticides with residual action* continue to kill adult parasites for a prolonged period of time. An example of a synthetic plant derivative is permethrin. Organophosphate insecticides with prolonged residual action are chemicals with names such as *carbaryl, chlorpyrifos,* and *propoxur.* Various manufacturers frequently give different brand names to the same or very similar chemicals.
- *Insect growth regulators (IGRs)* prevent parasite eggs from hatching. *Fenocarb, Precor,* and *Biolar* are some of these chemicals.
- *Combination products* contain both drugs that kill quickly and drugs with residual action to keep on killing. Some combination products contain insecticides and insect growth regulators to attack parasites in all stages of their life cycles.

NONPRESCRIPTION FLEA-CONTROL PRODUCTS

The market for flea- and tick-control preparations includes a vast and confusing array of new chemicals. Many of the products contain the same or very similar chemicals. Identical products may sell for very different prices. Owners are cautioned to compare ingredients and prices before making their selections. Unless the label states that the product can be used with other types of flea control, use only one product at a time.

Owners may find it difficult to make choices among the different forms of medications. Personal preference and convenience are factors to be considered when selecting a product.

Liquid preparations: dips, sprays, and shampoos

Dips are concentrated chemicals that are diluted with water and applied to the entire dog by immersing it in the dilute solution or by sponging the solution over its body. It is very important to follow the *exact* directions for mixing each dip. Mixed too strong, dips can be harmful; mixed too weak, dips can be ineffective. The use of dips is probably the most economical, effective method of controlling external parasites on dogs. See page 47 for tips on using dip.

Sprays are liquids supplied in pressurized cans or pump-top dispensers. Sprays are applied all over the body of the dog at full strength. Relatively quiet pump-top dispensers are more easily used on dogs that may be frightened by the noise of a spray can.

Shampoos contain lathering agents and fragrances as well as insecticides to kill parasites. When shampoos are rinsed off, however, much of the residual antiparasitic action of the insecticides is also rinsed off.

Dips, Sprays, and Shampoos

CHEMICALS	SOME BRAND NAMES	LENGTH OF ACTION
Chlorpyrifos	DURSBAN DIP	28 days
d-Limonene	NATURE'S ANSWER™ DIP & SHAMPOO	"repeat as needed"
Pyrethrins	DEFEND SHAMPOO	"repeat as needed"
	FLEA STOP PYRETHRIN	"repeat as needed"

Dips, Sprays, and Shampoos (*continued*)

CHEMICALS	SOME BRAND NAMES	LENGTH OF ACTION
	RAID FLEA KILLER PLUS SPRAY	"repeat as needed"
Pyrethrins & piperonyl butoxide	HARTZ 2 IN 1 RID FLEA SHAMPOO	"weekly if needed"
Pyrethrins and precor	OVITROL PLUS DIP OVITROL PLUS SPRAY	Adult fleas: 7 days Flea eggs: 5 months
Permethrin	DEFEND DIP AND SHAMPOO	"weekly as needed"
Pyrethrins and permethrin	X-O-TROL SPRAY	"weekly as needed"
Phosmet	PARAMITE	fleas, ticks, mites: 9–16 days
Rotenone	HiLo DIP	"repeat as needed"
Pyrethrins and rotenone	DURAKYL PET DIP	"repeat as needed"

Powders

"Flea Powders" were the first preparations made for parasite control; powders are still a popular method of dealing with flea infection on dogs. The advantages of powders are that they are relatively inexpensive and relatively easy to apply. The disadvantage of powders is that they must be rubbed in to the skin to reach the parasites, they tend to sift off the animal into the environment, and powders usually do not contain chemicals that have a significant residual action.

Flea & Tick Powders

CHEMICAL	SOME BRAND NAMES	LENGTH OF ACTION
Carbaryl	VET-KEM	fleas: 7 days
Pyrethrins and carbaryl	FLEA STOP FLEA & TICK POWDER	fleas: 7 days

One-spot treatments

Systemic insecticides are chemicals that enter the dog's body and are dispersed through the dog's skin. Ectoparasites that feed on a treated dog are killed and/or their eggs are prevented from hatching. Systemic treatments are among the newest, most effective, and most easily used chemical parasite control for dogs.

One-spot products provide a measured amount of a chemical insecticide in little plastic tubes. The owner selects a dose appropriate to the dog's weight, snips the tip from the tube with a scissors, parts the dog's hair, and squeezes the chemical directly onto the dog's skin. The preferred sites of application are the back of the dog's neck or between the dog's shoulder blades—areas that are impossible for the dog to lick. Some products recommend that two containers of the medication be applied to large dogs, one on the back of the neck and one on the hip region. If the chemicals are applied in an area that the dog can lick, the dog must be prevented from doing so until the chemicals have dried.

A dog with an extremely thick undercoat such as the Chow should have a small area of skin exposed by removing the hair with a clipper or scissors before the product is applied. This will prevent a portion of the product from being wasted on the coat.

A few products for flea control are designed to be rubbed onto dogs' coats directly from the applicator bottle or from an insecticide-containing wax stick. The dose of chemicals applied by this method is not as accurate as is the dose of the products in individual one-dose tubes.

Not all one-spot products have the same action. Some contain insect growth regulators that prevent flea eggs from hatching, others contain long-lasting chemicals that kill adult fleas that bite the dog, and some contain both types of insecticides. This information is on the label of each product.

One-Spot Treatments

CHEMICAL	SOME BRAND NAMES	LENGTH OF ACTION
Permethrin and Biolar	BIO SPOT	adult fleas: 4 weeks eggs and larvae: 4 months
	DEFEND EXSPOT	adult fleas: 4 weeks
	HARTZ CONTROL FLEA HALT! SPOT-ON	adult fleas: 4 weeks
Chlorpyrifos	HAPPY JACK STREAKER INSECTICIDE	adult fleas: 14 days
Permethrin	HARTZ CONTROL ONE-SPOT	adult fleas: 4 weeks
Permethrin and Precor	POWER SPOT SPOT ON	adult fleas: 4 weeks adult fleas: 4 weeks
Nylar	FLEA SCIENCE SPOT ON	adult fleas: 4 weeks

Flea and tick collars

—

Children should not handle flea collars and then put their hands in their mouths. Another form of parasite control should be selected for dogs that are handled by small children.

—

Flea and tick collars consist of plastic bands impregnated with chemicals. The chemicals are slowly released from the plastic and act to kill adult parasites and larvae, and/or to prevent the parasite eggs from hatching. Most flea and tick collars have a residual action varying from six months to a year.

A correctly adjusted flea and tick collar is tight enough to be slipped off over the dog's head only with difficulty. A collar must not be applied so loosely that the dog can grasp it in its mouth. Excess length of the collar must be cut off with scissors and discarded. Growing puppies must have their collars inspected regularly and adjusted for their increase in size.

Several brands of flea and tick collars offer the owner a choice of white, blue, orange, or other colors. The colors of these products are merely decorative.

Flea and tick collars intended for puppies may contain the active ingredients in a lower concentration than collars intended for adult dogs. The ages for which each product is intended are clearly stated on the label.

Flea and tick collars are sold in sealed pouches to preserve their chemical action until the collars are put into use. Some flea and tick collars must be stretched to activate the release of chemicals.

Flea and Tick Collars

CHEMICAL	SOME BRAND NAMES	LENGTH OF ACTION
Diazinon	PREVENTIC FLEA COLLAR SULFODENE SCRATCHEX	adult fleas: 5 months
	FLEA & TICK COLLAR	adult fleas: 12 months
Chlorpyrifos (Dursban)	VET-KEM DURSBAN FLEA AND TICK COLLAR	adult fleas: 11 months ticks: 7 months
	VICTORY 12 FLEA & TICK COLLAR	adult fleas: 4 months

Flea and Tick Collars (*continued*)

CHEMICAL	SOME BRAND NAMES	LENGTH OF ACTION
	3X FLEA TICK AND MANGE COLLAR	adult fleas: 11 months ticks: 7 months
	12-MONTH METERED RELEASE COLLAR	adult fleas: 12 months ticks: 7 months
Diazinon	ENCORE FLEA & TICK COLLAR	adult fleas: 10 months, ticks 7 months
Permethrins	HiLo FLEA & TICK COLLAR	adult fleas: 3 months
Chlorpyrifos & Precor	ZODIAC POWER BAND	adult fleas & eggs: 11 months ticks: 5 months
Naled & Sendran	SARGENTS DUAL ACTION FLEA & TICK COLLAR	adult fleas: 5 months
Propoxur and Carbaryl	ZODIAC 5 MO. FLEA & TICK	adult fleas: 5 months
Pyriproxifen (Nylar)	KNOCKOUT IGR COLLAR	flea eggs & larvae: 15 months
Tetrachlor- vinphos	HARTZ 2-IN-ONE FLEA & TICK COLLAR	adult fleas: 5 months
	HARTZ CONTROL ULTIMATE FLEA COLLAR	7 months

Note: Flea collars are not always completely effective, especially on large dogs.

Chemicals for use in the house and yard

A number of chemicals are marketed to kill adult fleas, ticks, and larvae, and to prevent eggs from hatching in carpeting, dogs' bedding, kennels, and yards. Application of these products may be beneficial where parasites are very numerous. After control has been initiated, treatment of the animals alone should be sufficient.

Before a product is used, the label should be read very carefully. Some products designed for use in the environment are harmful if they come into contact with dogs. Another product contains living microscopic nematodes (worms) that devour preadult fleas in the soil. It is not advisable to use these products indoors.

Miscellaneous flea-control products

The market is full of devices that claim to kill, capture, or repel adult fleas. There is no indication that any of these products are effective. Owners are advised to use their money in more productive ways.

- *Electronic flea control tag:* "repels fleas with low-level ultrasonic pulse"
- *Ultrasonic pest repeller:* a device that plugs into an electric socket and "emits ultrasonic sounds that repel pests"
- *Overnight flea trap:* has a night-light that "attracts fleas," which stick to a glue board or fall into water
- *Natural herbal collars* that "repel fleas"
- *Flea combs* to remove fleas from animals' coats

10

OTHER ECTOPARASITES: TICKS, LICE, MANGE, AND RINGWORM

TICKS

Ticks are not insects. They are members of the family *Arachnida,* which includes spiders and mites. Ticks go through several stages of development, some on and some off their hosts. A tick feeds only when it is on a host animal. Ticks do not feed during the stages of its life cycle that are spent off a host animal.

The life cycle of the tick
• Adult ticks resemble small, fat eight-legged spiders. Various species differ in size; the male and unengorged female of the common brown dog tick (*Dermacentor variabilis*) are about one-eighth inch in length. Ticks mate on the host animal. The male tick is almost always found close to the female but is very small and hard to see.

• The female tick embeds her mouthparts in the skin of the host and gorges on the host's blood. An engorged female tick may be up to one-half inch in length. Its abdomen enlarges to the extent that its head and legs are relatively unnoticeable. When full of blood, a female tick resembles a dark round wart or tumor.

• After feeding, the female tick drops to the ground and lays hundreds of eggs. These eggs hatch in two weeks to several months, depending on the environmental temperature. Eggs laid in the fall may not hatch into larvae until the following spring.

• First-stage larvae are called *seed ticks* and have only six legs. They must find a host upon which to feed if they are to survive. Larval ticks are *negatively geotropic;* they crawl upward on blades of grass or twigs and await the passing of a suitable host. In a building infested with ticks, seed ticks crawl up cracks and corners in the walls. When alerted by the vibrations of passing animals, ticks can move with astonishing speed to gain access to the host animals' skin.

• Larval seed ticks attach their mouthparts to the skin of the host and feed upon its blood. After a few days or a week, the seed ticks drop off the host and change into the next stage, the *nymphs.* Nymphs are eight-legged like their parents, but are not sexually mature.

• Nymphal ticks are also negatively geotropic; they crawl upward to await the presence of another host. In some species of ticks, successive hosts must be of different species. In the brown dog tick, each host is usually the same species, often the same dog.

• The nymphs again feed, again drop off the host, and again undergo change. When they become adults, the ticks seek a final host upon which to mate and engorge with blood.

Tick eradication is important

The saliva of ticks does not have the same allergenic effect on dogs as does flea saliva. Dogs seldom scratch from even a heavy infestation of ticks. However, ticks are bloodsuckers, unattractive on dogs and certainly unattractive as seed ticks and nymphs crawling up the walls of a dwelling.

Ticks are also vectors of several zoonotic diseases. Rocky Mountain spotted fever, tick paralysis, and Lyme disease are among the diseases spread by ticks to dogs, humans, and other animals. Prevention and eradication of ticks should not be neglected just because infested dogs do not have significant pruritus.

• If possible, dogs should be kept out of tick-infested areas. In areas where ticks are prevalent, yards where dogs exercise should be treated with appropriate chemicals to kill adult and immature ticks.

• Dogs should be examined frequently for the presence of ticks on their bodies. Ticks prefer sheltered locations, such as inside the ears and between the toes of the host. A heavily infested dog may have ticks anywhere on its body. The larvae and nymphs of ticks are so small that they may be unnoticed until they have enlarged by feeding on the dog's blood. Inspection of a tick-infested dog must be done daily to find each new tick as it enlarges. Ticks can be removed by simply plucking them off the dog; if the tick mouthparts remain embedded in the dog's skin, these parts will dry up and fall off within hours. Alcohol or another suitable disinfectant may be applied to the site from which the tick was removed.

Since ticks may be the vectors of several diseases, it is unwise to pluck them off the dog's skin with bare hands. Forceps, tweezers, rubber gloves, or several layers of plastic wrap can be used to protect hands from contact with the ticks. Ticks can and will survive for long periods off a host. If the species of the tick is not known, it can be saved for identification by sealing it in an empty glass jar. Ticks that are not needed for identification should be flushed down the toilet.

• Many (but not all) products that are applied to dogs' skin to kill fleas will also be effective against ticks. Since ticks are not insects, products that contain only "insect growth regulators" will not disrupt the life cycles of ticks. Many preparations that are designed to kill both fleas and ticks contain more than one class of drugs.

Flea- and tick-killing preparations are available as spot-ons, sprays, dips, powders, collars, and products designed only for use in yards and kennels. Most of the newer synthetic insecticides will kill ticks; products that contain only pyrethrins are less effective. Ticks are more resistant to insecticides than are fleas, and may take longer to die from the application of chemicals that will kill fleas almost immediately. The residual action of drugs may be considerably shorter for ticks than for fleas.

Collars for Tick Control

CHEMICAL	SOME BRAND NAMES	LENGTH OF ACTION
Chlorpyrifos	FOSTER & SMITH FLEA AND TICK COLLAR	fleas: 12 months ticks: 6 months
Amitraz	TICK ARREST	75 days
	PREVENTIC	90 days

LICE

Lice are uncommon on dogs. *Linognathus piliferus* is the species occasionally found. These white, soft-bodied insects cause moderate itching to their hosts.

The life cycle of the louse

• Lice are entirely host-specific; the dog louse will not live on humans, the human louse will not live on dogs. The term for a human infestation with lice is *pediculosis*. If a child comes home from school with head lice, he caught them from a classmate, not from a dog.

• Lice spend their entire life cycle upon the body of the host. They mate on the dog and attach the eggs (called *nits*) to the hairs of the dog.

• Lice are transmitted from one animal to another by direct body contact or by contact with recently infested objects such as brushes and combs. Lice will die within hours if they are not on the body of a host.

Treatment of lice on dogs

Adult lice are easy to kill. Chemicals used in flea and tick preparations effectively kill lice. Synthetic insecticides have some residual action against newly hatched lice; the natural plant extracts—pyrethrins and rotenone—do not.

Insecticides do not kill the nits, nor are the nits removed from the hair shafts by ordinary bathing. Nits will hatch into new lice within a week. Frequent repeat treatments with insecticides are needed to eliminate them all.

Nits can be picked off with combs designed to remove them from human heads. Removing nits by hand is a tedious process, giving rise to the expression "nit-picking." Since nits are attached to the base of the hair shafts, shaving affected dogs will eliminate them. Clipping that allows any significant length of hair on the dog will leave the nits as well.

Preparations Designed for Human Use to Eliminate Lice (Can Be Used to Control Lice on Dogs)

CHEMICAL	SOME BRAND NAMES	COMMENTS
Permethrin	A-200 LICE CONTROL SPRAY	for humans' clothing & fleas and ticks on dogs

**Preparations Designed for Human Use to Eliminate Lice
(Can Be Used to Control Lice on Dogs) (*continued*)**

CHEMICAL	SOME BRAND NAMES	COMMENTS
	NIX CRÈME RINSE RID LICE CONTROL SPRAY	for bedding
Pyrethrins & piperonyl butoxide	CLEAR TOTAL LICE ELIMINATION SYSTEM	shampoo, lice egg remover, & nit comb
	PRONTO LICE TREATMENT	shampoo
Pyrethirins	MAXIMUM STRENGTH RID SHAMPOO	shampoo

MANGE

The term *mange* is often applied to any unattractive skin condition of dogs. Correctly, mange is a skin disease caused by one of several species of microscopic mites. Dogs are hosts of two types of mange mites: *Demodex* and *Sarcoptes*.

Sarcoptic mange

Cause: Sarcoptic mange of dogs is caused by a mite that is similar to the scabies mite of humans. The dog mite, *Sarcoptes scabiei*, will live temporarily on human skin. Humans who have close contact with *Sarcoptes*-infected dogs may develop an itchy red rash on their hands and arms. The rash disappears after a few days when the mites die because they are on an unsuitable host.

Signs: An important sign of infection with sarcoptic mites is constant, intense itching of the host without any observable cause. The skin of a dog or puppy harboring sarcoptic mites may look fine, but the animal scratches constantly. When an infection has been present for weeks, the patient will be covered with self-inflicted lesions from biting and scratching.

Sarcoptes mites are easily transmitted from dog to dog by direct contact. The mites will live only a few hours off the host; bedding and other objects are rarely sources of infection.

Diagnosis: When the mites are found in a skin scraping examined by a veterinarian under a microscope, the diagnosis is confirmed. Since *Sarcoptes* mites are not numerous on a host and may be hard to find, negative skin scrapings do not rule out the presence of this condition. A presumptive diagnosis of sarcoptic mange is logical if a puppy or young dog is scratching constantly and no fleas can be found. The diagnosis can be confirmed by the host's response to treatment.

Dogs with severe fleabite allergy are usually older animals that have had years of exposure to flea saliva. Puppies and young dogs that scratch constantly, apparently without harboring fleas, should be treated for *Sarcoptes* even without finding the mites in a skin scraping.

Treatment: The mite that causes sarcoptic mange is not hard to kill. OTC flea and tick dips containing 5 percent permethrin, OTC organophosphate dips, and several prescription medications (one of which is given orally) will eliminate *Sarcoptes* mites. Some of the products used against *Sarcoptes* may be toxic to young puppies and certain breeds of dogs; no product should be used except under strict compliance with the label directions or on the advice of a veterinarian.

Sarcoptic Mange Treatment

CHEMICAL	SOME BRAND NAMES	DELIVERY
Lindane	FLEA STOP FLEA & TICK DIP & MANGE CONTROL	liquid dip
	PARAMITE	liquid dip

Demodectic mange

Mange caused by the mite *Demodex canis* is entirely different in character from sarcoptic mange.

Small numbers of demodex mites are thought to be a normal part of the canine skin. Demodex mites on dogs live in the hair follicles of all parts of the body; they spend their entire lives on a single host.

Demodectic mange is not contagious in the usual sense. It is thought that puppies acquire the mites from their mother during the first few days of life. Transmission of demodex mites from a mother dog to her unborn puppies has not been demonstrated.

The skin of older animals is resistant to the invasion of demodex mites. Once a puppy is more than a few weeks of age, it cannot "catch" demodectic mange from another affected dog, nor can it transmit the condition to another dog, no matter how close their contact.

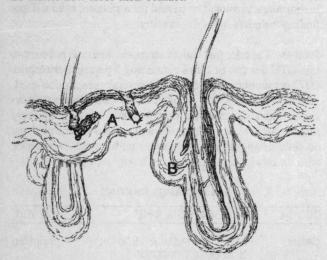

(A) Sarcoptic mange mites in burrows in the skin. (B) Demodectic mange mites inside a hair follicle.

Cause: The clinical disease of demodectic mange probably occurs when an impairment of the patient's immune systems allows the demodex mites to proliferate in the hair follicles. Few puppies less than three months of age have demodex lesions. Dogs that will be affected usually have signs of the disease before they are a year old. Some breeds are more likely to have demodex; the condition is common in some short-haired breeds such as the Doberman and the dachshund. An older dog that develops demodex lesions undoubtedly has had the mites in its hair follicles since it was very young.

Signs: Demodectic mange can take two forms: the *localized* and the *generalized.* The lesions of local demodex appear as small bald spots on puppies from four to twelve months of age, usually on the face around the eye and at the corners of the mouth, occasionally on the front feet. The lesions are not pruritic; the puppies do not scratch at them.

Most cases of localized demodex are self-limiting. They will disappear in thirty to sixty days without treatment or with only minimal treatment. In many cases, the application of topical medication is probably neither effective nor needed. If a puppy is observed to have only a few spots, the condition may resolve without treatment.

Cases of generalized demodectic mange begin as localized conditions, but spread over the entire bodies of affected dogs. Generalized cases of demodex are characterized by secondary bacterial infection and hair loss over the patient's body and limbs.

Diagnosis: A positive diagnosis of demodectic mange is made by finding the mites in a skin scraping examined under the microscope. Unlike sarcoptic mites, the demodex mites are numerous and easy to find, even in a very shallow scraping.

Therapy: If the lesions of localized demodex appear to be spreading, therapy should be started without delay. Treatment of generalized demodex with nonprescription drugs is very unlikely to be successful. Only a veterinarian can prescribe effective miticides to kill the mites and effective antibiotics to treat the secondary bacterial skin infection. A veterinarian may also prescribe steroids to reduce inflammation and drugs to boost the patient's immune system.

Months of treatment may be necessary to bring a severe case of generalized demodex under control. However, with modern prescription drugs, almost every case can be treated successfully. Euthanasia of severely affected dogs is rarely necessary if the owner is willing to spend the time, effort, and money to treat the dog.

RINGWORM

The term *ringworm* is used for this condition because the skin lesions often develop in a circular pattern. The causative organism, however, is a fungus, not a worm.

Human ringworm and animal ringworm are very similar, and in fact may be caused by the same organism. Ringworm organisms are transmissible both to humans and animals by contact with infected members of the same or different species.

Cause: *Microsporum canis* is the most common fungus that causes ringworm in both dogs and cats. Ringworm is more common in cats than it is in dogs. The disease may be present but not apparent in adult cats, but affected cats will transmit the ringworm organisms to their kittens. Human cases of ringworm caused by contact with infected pets are much more common in children than in adults, apparently because adults have greater resistance to the *Microsporum* organisms.

Diagnosis: The typical lesions of ringworm, both on humans and animals, are circular, raised, mildly itchy, red lesions that tend to spread from a central area outward on the skin. Early ringworm lesions on dogs are easily mistaken for localized demodectic mange lesions. The diseases are differentiated by laboratory tests.

Diagnosis of ringworm is made by several procedures. Examination with a Wood's light (a special ultraviolet light) will cause some ringworm organisms to show a characteristic yellow-green fluorescence. A negative Wood's light test does not rule out ringworm, since many ringworm organisms are not fluorescent.

In many cases, microscopic examination of chemically treated hair shafts will reveal the spores of ringworm organisms. The most accurate diagnostic method for fungi is a culture of samples of suspected hair or skin on a specially prepared preparation that will promote fungal growth.

A veterinarian must treat dogs with ringworm. Medication applied to the skin of an animal or human affected with ringworm is a vastly inferior treatment to systemic (oral) medications that are available only on the prescription of a physician or veterinarian.

———

Note: Under no condition should any OTC human topical preparations for ringworm or athlete's foot ever be applied to an animal. Not only are these agents ineffective, they are toxic if the animal licks them.

———

11

THE DIGESTIVE SYSTEM

The strongest instinct present in all members of the animal kingdom is to consume food. This instinct is basic to survival—an animal does not live if it does not eat—but can lead to much woe for both man and dog, at least partly because of indiscreet selection of items eaten.

Many dogs will eat anything even remotely organic, just as many dogs will consume all the food that they are able regardless of their need. What appears to be greed is a survival tactic; a wild carnivore never knew where its next meal was coming from. Domestic carnivores retain this instinct, often to their detriment.

The canine digestive tract does not function in exactly the same manner as does the human digestive tract. The differences are caused by anatomic and physiological variations between the species.

• By nature, dogs are carnivorous. Most of the diet of wild canines is made up of the meat, bones, and ingesta of their prey. Vegetarian owners must realize that their dogs require substances that are found only in meat. A dog restricted to a vegetarian diet will eventually develop a severe deficiency of essential amino acids.

• Because dogs are naturally hunters, gorging is a natural action. A hunting animal gorges on its prey and hunts again only when its digestive tract is empty. The wild carnivore may eat only once every few days.

• Dogs have no digestive enzymes in their saliva. Unlike humans, who chew their food, dogs (wild or domestic) tear their food into pieces just small enough to be swallowed, then gulp down the pieces. All dogs' digestive processes take place in the stomach and small intestines, none in the mouth. Occasionally a dog may consume material that is impossible or dangerous to pass. In this case, surgical treatment may be needed.

ANOREXIA (REFUSAL TO EAT)

Anorexia in dogs is not a disease in itself; it is a sign of another condition. Anorexia is a sign of a problem only when it is an unusual behavior in a dog. A dog that gradually eats less and less, especially if the dog also has a decrease in activity level or other signs such as vomiting and diarrhea, may be suffering from a chronic disease process. A dog that suddenly refuses its food is likely to be a victim of an acute disease or toxicity from something it has eaten.

There is a great deal of variation in healthy dogs' (and humans') natural appetites. Some dogs will eat anything that they are given or that they can steal. Some dogs will eat only the food to which they are accustomed. Some dogs refuse food that is not composed of or mixed with substances that they have learned to relish, such as meat. *Fussy eaters* are easy to identify: these dogs readily consume table food, treats, or canned all-meat products, but refuse ordinary dog food.

Owners of fussy eaters have two choices: they can cater to their dogs' whims and feed "people food" or other delicacies that their dogs favor, or they can provide a properly balanced diet at regular intervals and remove uneaten food after a few minutes. When training a dog to eat a balanced diet, owners must not offer anything at all from the table or as treats between meals. If the owners are persistent, their fussy eaters will eventually consume enough of the food to maintain good health.

Shy feeders are not fussy eaters; these are dogs that want to eat their food, but that are frightened by the presence of people, other animals, or situations in which they feel insecure. Shy feeders do best if fed in their kennels or in small, isolated, quiet spaces. A shy feeder often will accept food on a flat plate or a piece of newspaper that it would be reluctant to grab out of a deeper bowl. Shy feeders may be encouraged to eat by adding a small amount of "treat" food on top of their regular food; this practice should be discontinued as soon as the dog feels secure enough to consume a normal diet.

BLOAT (ACUTE GASTRIC DILATATION AND GASTRIC TORSION)

Bloat is the acute distention of the stomach with gas, fluid, food, or a combination of these substances. The condition occurs primarily in large breeds of dogs, although it has been seen in the smaller breeds. Bloated dogs can go into shock and die very quickly.

Two conditions can cause bloat. In cases of acute gastric dilatation, the stomach fails to empty because the esophageal and pyloric sphincters fail to function properly. In cases of gastric torsion, the stomach is actually rotated and turned over. This displacement effectively constricts both the entrance and exit to the organ, trapping food and gas within the stomach.

It has been postulated that bloat is caused by a hereditary abnormality, by eating large amounts of dry food, by certain dog food ingredients such as horsemeat or wheat products, or by excitement or strenuous activity following feeding. None of these factors is present in every case; no single factor can be implicated as the only cause of bloat. Since bloat may be caused by many conditions, no recommendations can be made for its prevention. Owners of susceptible breeds should learn to recognize the signs.

Bloat is an acute condition; it comes on very suddenly. Dogs usually show the first signs of bloat within a few hours of eating. A bloated dog has extreme abdominal distention, excess salivation, unproductive attempts to vomit, and signs of pain and shock. Every dog with bloat will not exhibit all these signs to the same degree.

The treatment of a bloated dog includes immediate surgery to relieve the distention and intravenous fluid to combat shock. **There are no oral medications, prescription or nonprescription, that will save the life of a dog with this condition.**

———

Bloat is an emergency. If signs of bloat are present, the dog must be rushed to an emergency hospital for treatment. Without treatment, a bloated dog can die in a few hours.

———

CONSTIPATION

A constipated dog strains to move its bowels and produces small, hard stools or nothing at all. As with vomiting and diarrhea, constipation can be acute or chronic.

Acute constipation

The eating of bones or other indigestible material is the most common cause of acute constipation in the dog. These materials produce bulky, dry stools that the dog cannot easily pass. In severe cases, fragments of bones in the dog's colon can produce *obstipation,* a condition in which the entire lower bowel is blocked. Obstipation requires veterinary attention and often requires that the dog be anesthetized or tranquilized while the obstruction is removed.

Constipation in puppies

After being treated with a medication to eliminate parasitic worms, a heavily parasitized puppy may pass only a portion of a large mass of worms; the rest of the mass may have to be removed manually from the puppy's anus, one worm at a time.

Acute constipation in long-haired puppies such as poodles may occur if inattentive owners do not notice that masses of stool and hair have adhered to the puppies' anal areas and effectively sealed off the anus. An affected puppy strains and cries, but cannot defecate. The masses of fecal material can be removed more easily if softened by warm running water. The skin under the fecal mat is often badly irritated by the condition. Since the dermatitis in this area is moist, the application of a drying agent such as antiseptic powder is indicated. Problems caused by masses of feces and hair surrounding the anus can be prevented (and cured) by the *careful* use of scissors or a clipper.

Puppies that eat foreign material may strain to pass it. Mineral oil administered in food may help alleviate the situation. Veterinary attention is needed if the material contains objects that might penetrate the bowel.

Occasional constipation

As do humans, dogs suffer occasionally from constipation caused by insufficient moisture in their diet or by eating indigestible materials. Human stool softeners containing *docusate sodium* are safe for dogs when used in appropriate doses. Capsules are available in pediatric and adult sizes. *Milk of magnesia* is another safe laxative for dogs; the tablets are easily administered in a piece of food. *Mineral oil* and other liquid or oily medications must not be spooned down a dog's throat. If the material is accidentally inhaled, it may cause lung damage. Most dogs will eat mineral oil or other liquids if offered on a slice of bread or mixed with a small amount of tasty food.

—

Dogs should not be given human stimulant laxatives such as castor oil or chocolate laxative preparations.

—

Chronic constipation

Most cases of chronic constipation occur in older dogs and have the same cause as chronic constipation in older humans: insufficient bulk and insufficient moisture intake in the diet. The condition is not uncommon in sedentary house dogs that are fed dry food and receive little exercise.

Fecal masses that remain too long in the lower bowel may become dry, hard, and difficult to pass. Exceptionally well housebroken dogs may become constipated from insufficient opportunity to move their bowels out of doors. A dog may also be reluctant to move its bowels because of pain in the anal area from impacted anal sacs, perianal fistulas, or other abnormal conditions. Enlargement of the prostate in male dogs may cause defecation to be difficult and painful. Any of these conditions can result in chronic constipation in dogs and will require veterinary treatment.

The cause of chronic constipation should be determined and corrected. In most cases, a change to a diet higher in bulk is indicated. Soaking dry dog food before feeding will often supply enough moisture in the dog's intestines to alleviate the problem. Bulk in the form of bran cereal added to the dog food is often beneficial. Bran flakes or granules can be added at the rate of a tablespoonful for each cup of food the dog receives; this amount should be increased gradually until the desired results are obtained. Many dogs that tend to become constipated can be maintained indefinitely on a diet of dog food with added bran. Bulk-producing human laxatives that instruct the patient to take them with or in a glass of water or fruit juice should not be used in the dog, since it is not possible to assure that a dog will drink the required amount of liquid.

Human nonprescription laxatives are of three types: bulking agents, fecal softeners, and bowel stimulants. Only fecal softeners are appropriate for treating constipation in dogs.

Human laxative products that contain bulk-producing agents such as methylcellulose and psyllium require that each dose be taken with eight ounces of water or fruit juice. When mixed with water, these medications are not attractive to dogs; very few dogs will voluntarily lap up the product. Since it is not possible to ensure that a dog will consume the medication in compliance with the label instructions, bulk-producing commercial laxatives are not recommended for dogs.

Dogs' digestive systems do not function exactly as do human digestive systems. Human laxatives that stimulate intestinal motility may be harmful to dogs and should never be given.

Human Laxatives that Are Safe for Dogs

CHEMICAL NAME	SOME BRAND NAMES	HOW SUPPLIED	DOSE
Docusate sodium	COLACE	capsules of 50 or 100 mg syrup, 20 mg per tsp. drops, 10 mg per ml	under 10 lb b.w.: 20 mg 10–25 lb b.w.: 50 mg 25–50 lb b.w.: 100 mg over 50 lb b.w.: 200 mg
	CORRECTOL STOOL SOFTENER	100-mg soft-gels	
	PHILLIP'S LIQUI-GELS	100-mg capsules	

Directions: Administer the capsules or soft-gels in food.

| *Magnesium hydroxide* | PHILLIP'S MILK OF MAGNESIA | liquid, 400 mg per tsp | 10–25 lb b.w.: 1 tsp.
25–50 lb b.w.: 2 tsp.
over 50 lb b.w.: 1 to 2 tbs. |

Human Laxatives that Are Safe for Dogs (*continued*)

CHEMICAL NAME	SOME BRAND NAMES	HOW SUPPLIED	DOSE
Mineral oil	generic liquid		under 10 lb b.w.: ½ tsp. 10–25 lb b.w.: 1 tsp. 25–50 lb b.w.: 1 tbs. over 50 lb b.w.: 2 tbs.

Directions: Administer on food. Do not combine with other laxatives.

COPROPHAGIA (EATING STOOLS)

Stool eating does not indicate that a dog lacks vitamins, minerals, or anything else in its diet. Stool eating is merely an unattractive habit.

Some dogs will eat their own stools, some will eat the stools of other dogs, and most stool eaters will eat any stools they can find. Dogs seldom eat dried stools, but many dogs that never eat stools in the summer relish frozen ones in the winter.

Coprophagia is a learned behavior, promoted by allowing the dog contact with stools in a dirty run or kennel yard. Once the habit is established, it is very hard to break. Obviously, the first procedure in preventing coprophagia is to keep runs and yards clean.

Commercial products are available that claim to make the stools distasteful to the dog. Not every dog is deterred from coprophagia by the use of these products. Those that are deterred will start to eat stools again when the use of the product is discontinued. The addition of commercial meat tenderizers to dog food is supposed to "digest" the attractive undigested elements in dogs' stools. This has not been proven effective in curbing the habit.

Nearly all dogs will eat cat stools, since cat stools smell like cat food. The solution to this problem is to locate cats' litter boxes out of dogs' reach.

Drugs to Prevent Coprophagia (Stool Eating)

PRODUCT	BRAND NAME	HOW SUPPLIED	DOSE
Natural vegetable extracts	DETER	powder packets	1 packet per 10 lb b.w.
	FOR-BID	powder packets	1 packet per feeding
	DIS-TASTE	tablets	1 tablet per 10 lb b.w.

Directions: sprinkle on food or crumble tablets on food.

—

Note: These products can be purchased at pet stores and through pet supply catalogs. These and similar products do not always work as advertised. Commercial meat-tenderizer powders (displayed in grocery stores with the spices) also contain "vegetable extracts" and have been used to prevent coprophagia, also with variable results.

—

DIARRHEA

Any stool of a dog that is not solid enough to hold a shape is considered to be diarrhea. This can range from merely soft stool to completely liquid feces. Diarrhea is a sign of a disturbance of the small and/or large intestine. As with vomiting, diarrhea can be a sign of a severe, life-threatening condition, a sign of simple overeating, or a sign of anything in between.

Danger signs accompanying diarrhea are similar to those accompanying vomiting:

- The diarrhea is of sudden onset. Vomiting is also present.
- The patient is depressed, inactive, and evidences abdominal pain.
- The stool is very watery, bloody, or foul smelling.
- The patient refuses food and may have an elevated body temperature.
- The condition lasts more than twenty-four hours.
- The patient strains unproductively to move its bowels.

—

If any of these signs are present a veterinarian should see the dog within a few hours

—

As with humans, dogs can get diarrhea from far less serious conditions than life-threatening disease. The dog with diarrhea that wants to eat and is normally active is probably suffering from eating something it should not have eaten such as the cat's food, the neighbor's garbage, or greasy table scraps.

Diarrhea in puppies

Diarrhea in puppies that have been vaccinated or that have not been exposed to contagious disease is usually caused by overfeeding or by intestinal parasites. Many puppies are such greedy eaters that they never should be fed all the food they will consume at one time. If a puppy is normally active but has diarrhea, it should be fed smaller quantities at each meal. Very occasionally a puppy will have diarrhea from sensitivity to its food; the other two causes are much more common.

Parasite infection is a very common cause of diarrhea in puppies. Unless the actual parasites can be seen in the stool or vomitus, an examination of the patient's fecal material under a microscope must be done to ascertain if parasites are present, to identify the species of parasite, and to determine the correct treatment. Repeated fecal examinations may be needed to detect parasites.

Intractable diarrhea in puppies with consistently negative fecal exams may warrant treatment for giardia even if the organisms cannot be found. See page 161 for a discussion of giardia.

Severe or chronic diarrhea in puppies can result in significant, even life-threatening dehydration. The presence of watery stools in young dogs is a condition that must not be neglected even for twenty-four hours. A veterinarian is needed to determine the cause of the condition and to institute corrective measures. Puppies at risk of dehydration can be given oral human or canine pediatric rehydration solutions, such as Pedialyte.

Diarrhea caused by excitement

Many dogs will have diarrhea when excited. Field-trial dogs commonly have loose bowel movements under the stress of training or competition; the condition is considered to be normal by their handlers. When not in a working situation, these dogs' stools will be formed. Diarrhea caused by excitement needs no treatment unless a dog consistently defecates in a vehicle. A change in the feeding schedule may alleviate this problem.

Simple diarrhea in mature dogs

If given the opportunity, most dogs will eat more than they should and will eat spoiled food, dead animals, and other decaying organic material. Feeding large amounts of fatty table scraps such as the Thanksgiving turkey skin will cause most dogs to have loose stools. Diarrhea in a dog that is not listless and that still wants to eat can be assumed to be caused by some dietary indiscretion of this type.

Dogs with simple diarrhea can be treated just as humans with the same condition. The safest treatment for simple diarrhea is the withholding of food for twelve to twenty-four hours until the condition corrects itself. Certain human antidiarrhea preparations such as *Kaopectate, Bismuth,* and antispasmodic medications can be administered to a dog if the doses are adjusted to the dog's size.

Drugs to treat simple diarrhea in dogs

Nonprescription Human Drugs that are Safe to Use to Treat Diarrhea in Dogs

CHEMICAL NAME	SOME BRAND NAMES	HOW SUPPLIED	DOSE
Attapulgite	KAOPECTATE	liquid	10–25 lb b.w.: ½ tbs.
			25–50 lb b.w.: 1 tbs.
			Over 50 lb b.w.: 2 tbs.
		Caplet	10–25 lb b.w.: ½ cap.
			25–50 lb b.w.: 1 cap.
			Over 50 lb b.w.: 2 caps.

Directions: One dose after each loose bowel movement. Maximum of 6 doses in 24 hours. Capsules should be swallowed whole.

Loperamide HCl	IMMODIUM AD	liquid	10–25 lb b.w.: 1 tsp.
			Over 25 lb b.w.: 2 tsp.

Nonprescription Human Drugs that are
Safe to Use to Treat Diarrhea in Dogs (*continued*)

CHEMICAL NAME	SOME BRAND NAMES	HOW SUPPLIED	DOSE
	IMMODIUM AD	caplet & chewable	10–25 lb b.w.: ½ cap.
			25–50 lb b.w.: 1 cap.

Directions: One dose after each loose bowel movement. Maximum of 4 doses in 24 hours. Not recommended for dogs under 10 pounds.

CHEMICAL NAME	SOME BRAND NAMES	HOW SUPPLIED	DOSE
Bismuth subsalicylate	PEPTO-BISMOL	liquid, tablets, & caplets	under 25 lb b.w.: ½ tab.
			25–50 lb b.w.: 1 tab.
			Over 50 lb b.w.: 2 tabs.

Directions: One dose after each loose bowel movement. Maximum of 8 doses in 24 hrs. Tablets are supposed to be chewed, caplets swallowed whole.

Diarrhea caused by parasites can be treated successfully only with an appropriate vermifuge. Some parasites cannot be eliminated with nonprescription drugs. Some can be treated with nonprescription medications.

EATING GRASS

Most dogs eat grass at one time or another, then will come into the house and vomit it onto the rug. Dogs do not eat grass because there is something wrong with them. The statement that dogs eat grass because they "need to vomit" has no more basis in fact than the statement that dogs eat grass because they "need to stain the rug."

The simple fact is that dogs occasionally like to eat grass but that grass is irritating to dogs' stomachs. The simple solution to the problem is to prevent dogs from eating grass; if this is not possible, leave them outside until they have vomited the grass.

FLATULENCE (INTESTINAL GAS)

Unfortunately, flatulence is a normal occurrence in the canine. The source of flatulence is bacterial action on undigested food particles in the dog's intestines.

If the condition is extremely offensive, an owner can try several remedies.

• *A change in diet.* Low-quality "generic" dog foods may contain lower-quality ingredients that are less digestible than the ingredients in better-formulated diets. "Premium" foods designed to be low in residue may reduce the amount of undigested material upon which intestinal bacteria act. "Senior" dog foods are formulated to be lower in total calories per unit of food; these products may be higher in bulking agents and may actually promote flatulence.

• *Elimination of foods containing gas-producing substances.* Some dogs have been improved when fed a diet that substitutes rice for wheat in the formula.

• *A change in feeding and exercise management.* The dog that is fed only in the morning and that receives adequate exercise is likely to pass less gas at night while lying next to its owner's chair.

• *The addition of specific digestive "aids."* Flatulence originates both in the small and large intestines. Human products that contain simethicone act by dispersing the trapped gas in the gastrointestinal tract. Products containing activated charcoal are intended to absorb intestinal gas. Products that are advertised as "enzyme dietary supplements" may produce a remarkable decrease in flatulence. Since humans and dogs vary widely in size, the dosage of these products must be determined by experimentation. As a general rule, dogs of 50 pounds or more will show improvement if given an adult human dose.

Drugs Used to Treat Flatulence (Intestinal Gas) in Dogs

CHEMICAL NAME	SOME BRAND NAMES	HOW SUPPLIED	DOSE
Alpha-D-galactosidase	BEANO	drops, tablets	under 25 lb b.w.: 5 dr. or 1 tab.
			over 25 lb b.w.: 10–15 dr. or 2–3 tab.

Directions: 5 drops equals one tablet. Should be dropped (or crumbled) onto food.

CHEMICAL NAME	SOME BRAND NAMES	HOW SUPPLIED	DOSE
Simethicone	GAS-X	chewable tablet	under 25 lb b.w.: 1 tab
			Over 25 lb b.w.: 2 tabs
	INFANT'S MILICON	drops	under 10 lb b.w.: 0.3 cc
			10 to 20 lb b.w.: 0.6 cc
	PHAZYME	liquid	under 25 lb b.w.: 1 tsp.
			Over 25 lb b.w.: 2 tsp.

Directions: Drop or crumble tablets on food. For small dogs, use Infant's Milicon which has a calibrated dropper in bottle.

Drugs Used to Treat Flatulence (Intestinal Gas) in Dogs (continued)

CHEMICAL NAME	SOME BRAND NAMES	HOW SUPPLIED	DOSE
Alumina, magnesia, and simethicone	EXTRA STRENGTH MAALOX	liquid or tablets	Under 50 lb b.w.: 1 tab. or 2 tsp. Over 50 lb b.w.: 2 tab. or 4 tsp.

Directions: For large dogs: mix with food or crumble tablets on food.

Simethicone and activated charcoal	CHARCOAL PLUS	tablets	1 or 2 tab. after meal
	FLATULEX	tablets	1 or 2 tab. after meals

Note: May cause dark stools.

OBESITY

One and only one condition causes obesity: *the consumption of more calories than are used by the body.* Excess calories are stored in the body as fat in humans as well as in other animals.

Obesity is recognized as a significant health hazard to humans, and it is an equally significant hazard to the health and longevity of dogs. The spaying and neutering of dogs reduces their activity level and caloric needs only very slightly. Spaying and neutering are not valid excuses for permitting dogs to be overweight.

It is much easier to prevent obesity than to cure it. Owners should judge their dogs' body conditions and feed them according to the dogs' needs, not the dogs' wishes or the "guidelines" printed on the bag of dog food.

The diet of a dog that is significantly obese should be reduced by 30 percent of the total calories until the dog approximates a normal weight. With sedentary house dogs, it will take six months or more for an obese dog to slim down. Every bite of table food and treat food must be taken into consideration when the total daily dietary intake is determined. "Lite," "senior," and "reducing" foods are available; these are usually only 20 to 30 percent lower in total calories than are regular dog foods. Feeding reduced-calorie food and feeding it in smaller amounts will accelerate a dog's rate of weight loss.

VOMITING

Dogs eat things that no normal human would consider to be food. Fortunately, dogs vomit much more readily than do humans, a fact that saves the lives of many a canine that finds and eats toxic substances.

Physiologically normal vomiting occurs in female dogs with litters of pups that are three or four weeks of age. Novice breeders have been horrified to see a bitch vomit her just-eaten meal in front of her puppies, and have been even more horrified to see the pups gobble up their mother's secondhand food. This entirely normal action is the method by which wild dogs start to wean their litters. Their pups learn to eat food that is torn into small pieces and partly digested before they are old enough to consume intact prey.

Simple vomiting in a mature dog results from eating indigestible or irritating material such as garbage or grass. The dog vomits once or twice, the offending material is eliminated from its stomach, then the dog appears to be perfectly normal. The dog does not have diarrhea and it continues to want its regular food. In cases such as this, no medication is needed. Food should be withheld for an hour or two after the dog has cleared its stomach by vomiting.

Vomiting in puppies can be caused by overeating. This is

most common in the largest, dominant members of a litter, which, in competition with their littermates, gobble up as much food as they can consume. The remedy is to feed the greedy puppies separately from the litter and to limit their food to a reasonable amount.

Vomiting in puppies can also be caused by roundworms in their stomachs. Parasitized puppies vomit at times other than after eating. The vomitus usually contains visible worms. The treatment is the administration of an appropriate worm medicine.

Megaesophagus is a congenital condition in which swallowed food cannot freely pass the esophageal sphincter and enter the stomach. The condition is present from birth but only becomes evident when young puppies begin to eat solid food. An affected puppy gulps down its food but immediately vomits it back, usually in a large, tube-shaped mass. Puppies with megaesophagus vomit *every time* after eating solid food; they are able to swallow liquids and may be able to swallow semiliquid preparations. A veterinarian must evaluate a puppy suspected of having megaesophagus. Methods of managing this condition include dietary, medical, and surgical treatments. Puppies may outgrow megaesophagus if handled appropriately.

Gastritis signifies an inflammation or irritation of the lining of the stomach. The most important sign of gastritis is vomiting. Gastritis in a dog can be the result of any condition from a life-threatening disease to a simple case of overeating. Prompt veterinary attention is needed if any of these danger signs are present:

- The dog is listless, inactive, and refuses food.
- The dog is unwilling to move and shows abdominal pain. These are the signs of a possible intestinal obstruction or serious disease.
- The dog wants to drink water, but vomits it shortly after drinking. The dog retches without vomiting. These

signs may indicate kidney disease, intestinal obstruction, or other serious conditions.

- The vomitus contains red blood or dark material that might be digested blood. The vomitus has an extremely objectionable odor. Vomiting blood can be a sign of a penetrating gastric or intestinal foreign body or of a disease such as parvovirus.
- Copious or bloody diarrhea is also present.
- The dog has a body temperature of greater than 103° F.
- The vomitus contains ascarids or other parasites.
- The dog continues to vomit for more than one day.

Occasional vomiting occurs in mature dogs that have the opportunity to find and eat indigestible material. The dog vomits only once or twice; the vomitus often contains pieces of the offending material that the dog has eaten. In these cases, the dog is not listless, not inactive, not anorexic, and does not have diarrhea.

The treatment of occasional vomiting caused by consumption of undesirable objects is simply to withhold food for twelve hours and allow the digestive system to eliminate the indigestible material.

An important diagnostic factor in determining the cause of vomiting is the time it occurs in relation to the time the patient has eaten. Dogs occasionally vomit a small amount of yellow or white foam when they anticipate being fed. This reaction is caused by the same reflex that caused Pavlov's dogs to drool when they anticipated food: not only do the salivary glands become active, but the stomach begins to produce acid digestive fluid, which is mildly irritating when the stomach is empty. This condition requires no treatment.

Vomiting caused by foreign bodies in the gastrointestinal tract

Complete or partial blocking of the gastrointestinal tract will cause vomiting and signs of pain. Foreign bodies that do not create blockage may also cause the same signs. Accurate diagnosis of these conditions can be made only by a veterinarian, usually by the use of X rays.

Vomiting related to other disease conditions

Cases of intractable or continued vomiting require veterinary attention. Uncontrolled vomiting that accompanies other disease conditions such as kidney failure may be treated with prescription medications from veterinarians.

It is not advisable to give human antiemetics unless the cause of the dog's vomiting is understood. However, continuous vomiting will result in dehydration of the patient. Solutions of phosphorated carbohydrates are nonprescription medications that can be used to treat vomiting without risk of harm.

Antiemetics (drugs to treat vomiting) that are safe for dogs

To Prevent Motion Sickness

CHEMICAL NAME	SOME BRAND NAMES	HOW SUPPLIED	DOSE
Meclizine	BONINE	25 mg chewable tabs	Under 50 lb b.w.: ½ tab.
	DRAMAMINE LESS DROWSY FORMULA	25 mg tablets	Over 50 lb b.w.: 1 tab.

Directions: Administer once in a 24-hour period.

Dimenhydrinate	DRAMAMINE	50 mg tablets	Under 50 lb b.w.: ½ tab.
			Over 50 lb b.w.: 1 tab. every 8 hours
	DRAMAMINE	12.5 mg per tsp. liquid	Under 20 lb b.w.: 1 tsp.

To Prevent Motion Sickness (*continued*)

CHEMICAL NAME	SOME BRAND NAMES	HOW SUPPLIED	DOSE
			20–50 lb b.w.: 2 tsp. every 8 hours

Directions: Administer at least ½ hour before trip.

To Treat Unrelieved Vomiting

CHEMICAL NAME	BRAND NAME	HOW SUPPLIED	DOSE
Phosphorated carbohydrate	EMETROL	liquid	1 or 2 tbs. as needed

Directions: May be administered every 30 minutes.

To cause vomiting if needed

Occasionally it is necessary to purposely cause a dog to vomit. Examples of this situation are *immediately* after a dog has swallowed a pair of diamond earrings or has consumed an entire package of a human's prescription medication. A teaspoonful of 3 percent hydrogen peroxide applied to the back of the tongue will produce vomiting within seconds.

CHEMICAL NAME	HOW SUPPLIED	DOSE
Hydrogen peroxide (3% solution)	liquid	1 tsp.
Baking soda (sodium bicarbonate)	powder	1 tsp.

Directions: Apply to back of tongue. May be repeated in 10 minutes.

12

WORMS AND OTHER INTERNAL PARASITES

"It must have worms" is the layman's time-honored diagnosis for whatever ails his dog. And in truth, intestinal parasites—"worms"—cause a great deal of sickness, debility, and occasionally death in dogs, especially in puppies and young dogs.

Many dogs that harbor internal parasites have no signs of infestation; the parasites are too few in numbers or the host is able to withstand their damage. However, internal parasites often are the cause of diarrhea, loss of body condition, dehydration, and blood loss, all of which can be extremely detrimental to the host.

DIAGNOSIS OF INTERNAL PARASITES

Many parasites cause the same universal sign: diarrhea of various degrees of severity and consistency.

A positive diagnosis of a specific parasite can only be made under certain conditions.

- The parasites or parts of the parasites appear in the stool, the vomitus, or attached to the hair around the tail of the host.
- The ova (eggs) of the parasites or the parasites themselves can be found by microscopic examination of the stool of the host.

Even if parasites or their ova are not found, the host may still have worms. Parasite eggs may be absent or too few in number at the time the sample was taken. Certain parasites are difficult to find in stool samples, since the ova of some parasites are not passed in the stool, and some parasites are too fragile to survive for long in a stool. Several stool examinations over a period of days or weeks (possibly performed by more than one method) must be done before an animal is considered to be free of internal parasites.

TREATMENT OF INTERNAL PARASITES

Worm medicines are poisons that must kill worms but must not kill the host as well. Successful worm medicines are those that kill or eliminate worms without doing any appreciable harm to the dog.

For generations, owners have used nonprescription medications to treat animal parasitism. Every farmer had his favorite "cure" for the "worms" that infected his livestock. Often these cures were substances that caused violent purging, thus eliminating some of the parasites by mechanical means alone. The owner who saw worms in his animal's diarrhea stools became convinced that his treatment was effective.

Modern drugs act in much more pleasant ways to eliminate parasites, often by interfering with the parasites' metabolism and thus causing their death. Only a few safe and effective OTC vermifuges are available. Many more parasitic infections of dogs are treated more safely and more effectively by the use of prescription medications. *The correct diagnosis and appropriate treatment of internal parasites requires more than merely administering a dose of "one-shot worm medicine" purchased at a drugstore.*

The action of nonprescription and prescription vermifuges

Nonprescription, over-the-counter canine vermifuges act to paralyze or partially paralyze the parasites. This enables the dog's normal intestinal movements to pass them in its stool.

Several nonprescription vermifuges rely on their severe purging action to aid in the elimination of the parasites.

All over-the-counter canine vermifuges are drugs that have been in use for many years. Veterinary science has developed many new prescription drugs that eliminate parasites much more thoroughly and without the unpleasant side effects of some of the older drugs. For example, a dog infected with tapeworms can be fasted for twelve hours, then given the traditional nonprescription drug *arecoline hydrobromide*. This drug partially paralyzes the tapeworms and greatly increases the dog's intestinal motility. The dog will experience severe straining and will have many watery stools containing the parasites. The dog may need to be treated again to eliminate those tapeworms that resisted the first treatment.

The same dog infected with tapeworms can be given the prescription drug *praziquantel* (Dronsit) in tablet form or by injection. Praziquantel destroys the ability of the tapeworm to resist the digestive enzymes in the dogs' intestines. No fasting is needed or recommended. The dog will have no diarrhea or straining. Few if any disintegrated tapeworm segments will be seen in the dog's stool. The dog will not need to be retreated unless it becomes infected with tapeworms again.

Piperazine is a safe and effective drug for treating roundworms in puppies. For the treatment of other internal parasites of dogs, modern prescription vermifuges are often the best choice.

If you do wish to try an OTC worm medication, the brand names mentioned in the charts are the more common products of their type. Each drug can be purchased in several forms and strengths.

The dose of every OTC vermifuge is determined by the weight of the dog to which the drug will be given. Directions for determining the correct dose are on the label of each product. Every dog should be weighed before its dose is calculated; in no instance should a dog be given a dose that is in excess of the recommended dose.

ASCARIDS (ROUNDWORMS)

"Puppy worms" and "stomach worms" are other names for these most common worms in puppies and young dogs.

Adult roundworms may be several inches long and large enough to be seen easily in the stool or vomitus of infected animals. They are called *roundworms* because they are round in cross section, as is a piece of spaghetti. The females are larger and thicker than are the males. Roundworms are passed in the stool or vomited spontaneously by heavily infested dogs, usually puppies. The worms are also passed soon after the animals are treated with a vermifuge. When first passed, the worms are motile.

Toxocara canis is the common roundworm found in dogs. *Toxascaris leonina* is another species often harbored by dogs. Humans have their own species of roundworm, *Ascaris lumbricoides,* a species that they share with swine.

Diarrhea is the most common and prevalent sign of roundworm infection in puppies. Heavily infected puppies may be seriously harmed or even killed by diarrhea-induced dehydration, by mechanical obstruction of their intestines, and by tissue damage caused by roundworm larvae.

Roundworms or their eggs are seldom found in the stools of mature, nonpregnant dogs. Apparently the adult dog's immune system causes the elimination of the worms in the dog's intestinal tract. However, roundworm larvae may remain as cysts in the dog's tissues throughout its life.

Most puppies are born infected with roundworms. They are infected in the uterus by larval roundworms that cross the placenta from the tissues of the mother dog. Puppies also become infected with roundworms when they ingest larval roundworms with their mother's milk, or when they ingest roundworm eggs from their contaminated environments.

Treatment of the mother, either before or during her pregnancy, will not eliminate the larvae that enter the puppies' bodies.

Some of the roundworms larvae that infest puppies do not develop into adults, but become cysts within the dog's tissues. These encysted worms are not affected by treatment that eliminates the adult parasites; the cysts remain in the dog's tissues. When a female dog becomes pregnant, these cysts become activated and develop into migrating larvae. Some of the larvae will cross the placenta and enter the puppies; some of the larvae will invade the mammary glands and be excreted with the milk; some will become adults in the female dog's intestines.

Roundworm larvae migrate throughout their hosts' bodies in the process of becoming adults in the intestines of the host. The larval forms of roundworms enter the pups before birth or when they nurse. These larvae migrate through the pups' tissues, especially the liver and lungs. Roundworm larvae cause tissue damage. Adult roundworms cause mechanical irritation and blockage of the intestinal tract, accompanied by severe diarrhea.

When larval roundworms reach the intestinal tracts of the mother and the puppies, they become adults. They mate and produce thousands of eggs that are passed in the stools of the puppies and the mother dog.

Roundworm eggs are microscopic in size and are produced in such vast numbers that the environments and coats of affected animals are contaminated with these eggs in various stages of development. When the eggs have developed to the infective stage, any animal that accidentally ingests them is subject to become infected with roundworms.

Humans may be infected. Even though the common dog roundworm, *Toxocara canis,* is not a human parasite and will not develop into adult roundworms in human intestines, the larvae of the dog roundworm will migrate through human tissues. These larvae may cause significant damage if they enter the organs, the brain, or the anterior chamber of the eye. *Visceral larval migrans* and *occular larval migrans* are conditions that may be found in children who put contaminated objects or dirty hands into their mouths.

Larval roundworm infections in children in the United States are not common. A few hundred cases are reported annually; probably many more cases are not diagnosed or not reported. Precautions taken to prevent roundworm larvae from affecting humans are also effective in minimizing the roundworm burden of puppies.

The sources of infection with roundworms are pregnant dogs, nursing dogs, and puppies. All should be treated repeatedly, even if microscopic examinations of their stools are negative for the parasite. Many well-cared-for mother dogs have so few roundworms to pass to their puppies that repeated stool checks may not detect them. Remember that a "few" is still too many; every female and every litter should be treated.

• Female dogs should be treated for roundworm infection after the first month of pregnancy and again two weeks before whelping. Treating female dogs before they are pregnant will not be effective in eliminating all roundworms.

• Mother dogs should be treated at two-week intervals while they are nursing. Adult roundworms may not be visible in the stool as a result of these treatments if the worms are eliminated before they become large enough to be noticed.

• Puppies should be treated as soon as their eyes open, and again every two weeks until they are ten weeks of age. After they are ten weeks of age, they need to be treated only if microscopic examination of their stools reveal roundworm eggs.

• Whelping boxes and puppy pens must be kept as clean as possible. Fecal material should be removed often. Puppies should be washed if they become dirty.

• Children (and adults) should be cautioned to wash their hands every time after they handle puppies or the mother dog.

Obviously, if puppies are to be treated at two weeks of age and mother dogs during late pregnancy, the drug used must be extremely nontoxic to the host. Piperazine is the only nonprescription drug safe to use against roundworms in very young puppies and in pregnant dogs. This drug has a wide margin of safety and is available in OTC form at pet and feed stores. Piperazine will affect *only* roundworms; it will not eliminate hookworms, tapeworms, or any other intestinal parasite.

Every dog and puppy to which any drug, including piperazine, is administered must be weighed before the dose of the drug is determined. No matter how safe a drug is, overdosing must be avoided.

Many veterinarians recommend prescription drugs for use in pregnant dogs and young puppies. These drugs are equally as safe as OTC roundworm medications and also are effective against several other internal parasites in addition to roundworms.

Note: Human medications prescribed for the removal of pinworms and ascarids in children are not the same as medications given for the treatment of parasites in dogs. **Human antiparasitic medications should not be given to dogs.**

Nonprescription Drugs for the Treatment of Roundworms (Ascarids) Only

CHEMICAL NAME OF DRUG	SOME BRAND NAMES	HOW SUPPLIED
Piperazine citrate or piperazine phosphate	PIPCIDE TABLETS	tablets
	TASTY PASTE	paste syringe
	PIPERAZINE TABLETS,	generic tablets
	PIPERAZINE LIQUID	generic liquid

Directions: No fasting required. This drug has a wide margin of safety. May be given to pregnant and nursing females and puppies as young as two weeks of age.

COCCIDIA

These parasites are not worms, they are microscopic proto-zoan organisms that live and reproduce within the epithelial cells of the host's intestine. Both the *Eimeria* genus and the *Isospora* genus are common in dogs and cats, and can be shared between the two. Dog and cat coccidia are not human parasites.

As with most intestinal parasite infections, diarrhea is the most common sign of the presence of coccidia. The diarrhea produced by coccidia is caused by the damage these para-sites inflict on the lining of the hosts' intestines. It may take more than a week for the diarrhea to improve even after the parasites are controlled. Puppies are most often and most se-verely affected; severe coccidial infection may result in pups' death from dehydration and intestinal damage. Coc-cidial infection should be suspected in puppies that have been treated for roundworms but that continue to have diar-rhea.

Infection with coccidia is by ingestion of the developed ova, called oocytes, from the environment. Diagnosis is confirmed by finding the tiny oocysts in stool samples examined under the microscope.

Treatment of coccidia is by administration of an oral medication for seven to ten consecutive days. Effective drugs are available by prescription only. Nonprescription vermifuges will not eliminate coccidia.

GIARDIA

Giardia is another species of microscopic protozoan organism that occupies the small intestine of several species of animals, including dogs and humans. These creatures damage the host when great numbers of them attach to the surface of the host's intestinal epithelium. They cause irritation to the lining of the intestinal tract, and mechanical obstruction of the absorption of nutrients and fluids by the host.

Infection with giardia is by ingestion of food—or more commonly, water—contaminated with the giardia cysts. *Giardia canis* found in dogs appears to be identical to *G. lamblia* found in humans. In experiments, dogs are easily infected with *G. lamblia;* presumably humans could be as easily infected with *G. canis.* Giardia infection, probably by the same organism, also occurs in cats and other mammals.

Giardia organisms are extremely difficult to find in a stool sample of an infected host. Infection with giardia should be suspected in animals with chronic, unresponsive diarrhea of unknown origin. If more than one species of mammal in a household are affected, a common source of infection such as a contaminated water supply should be suspected.

Only prescription drugs are effective in eliminating this parasite. If the parasites cannot be found in the stool, the diagnosis of giardiasis is often made by the dog's response to treatment.

HOOKWORMS

Adult hookworms are a quarter to a half inch in length, certainly visible to the naked eye but seldom passed as adults and difficult to see in the stool. The name *hookworm* comes from the curved, hook-shaped portion of this parasite. Although the infective larvae of the canine hookworm can cause a skin rash on people, humans and dogs do not share the same species of this parasite. The larvae of the dog parasite cannot become mature hookworms in humans.

Ancylostoma caninum is the common hookworm of the dog, although dogs can be infected with other species. Adult hookworms live in the small intestine of the host, where they become attached to the lining of the intestine and feed upon the host's blood and tissue fluids. A heavy infection with hookworms can cause enough blood loss in weak or young animals to produce severe anemia and even death.

Each female hookworm in the small intestine produces thousands of microscopic eggs that are passed in the stools of the hosts. The eggs require moisture and warmth to hatch into hookworm larvae. Larvae feed upon fecal material; if conditions are favorable, they develop into the infective stage in a week or less.

A puppy becomes infected with hookworms in one of three ways: it ingests material soiled with feces containing the infective larvae, it ingests the hookworm larvae with its mother's milk, or the larvae penetrate the host's skin and migrate through its tissues into its intestinal tract. Canine infection is likely to be through the oral route in puppies that are reared in contaminated environments. Human infection with *Ancylostoma duodenale* or *Necator americanus* is most likely to be through the skin in humans who walk barefoot in contaminated soil.

A diagnosis of hookworm is confirmed only by finding the ova in the dog or puppy's stool sample. Puppies with a heavy infestation of hookworms may not thrive; puppies with light infestations may have no signs of the parasite until their hookworm burden becomes overwhelming. Puppies' stools should be examined for hookworm ova by the time the pups are four weeks of age, and repeatedly until the pups are at least twelve weeks old.

Nonprescription medications are available that treat both hookworms and roundworms in dogs and puppies. These medications are of reasonable safety and efficacy if used strictly according to directions. Note: piperazine given for roundworm infections has no effect against hookworms.

Nonprescription Drugs for the Treatment of Roundworms and Hookworms

CHEMICAL NAME OF DRUG	SOME BRAND NAMES	HOW SUPPLIED
Pyrantel pamoate	NEMEX-2	tablets and liquid
	D-WORM	tablets and liquid
	SERGEANT'S SURE SHOT	liquid
	EVICT	liquid

Directions: No fasting required. May be given to puppies and pregnant and nursing females.

TAPEWORMS

Adult tapeworms are, as their name suggests, the shape of an elongated, flattened tape and can often be more than twelve inches in length. The head is at the thin end of the tape, while ripe segments full of eggs are found at the thick end.

The tapeworm is a two-host parasite. The common dog

tapeworm, *Dipylidium caninum,* is carried by fleas, while the rabbit is the intermediate host for the less common tapeworm, *Taenia pisiformis.* Since many more dogs have fleas than eat infected rabbits, it is easy to see why *Dipylidium caninum* is the more common organism.

Although humans have several species of tapeworm of their own, the intermediate hosts for most species of which are fish, there have been confirmed reports of children being infected with the dog tapeworm, *D. caninum.* It is thought that these children accidentally swallowed infected fleas.

A tapeworm consists of a head, or *scolex,* and numerous segments, the *proglottids.* The scolex contains most of the organism's organs, with the exception of the reproductive organs, which are contained in the proglottids. The tapeworm scolex becomes fastened to the mucous membranes of the host's small intestine, while proglottids continuously grow from the "neck." The youngest segment is the one closest to the head.

Each proglottid contains both male and female reproductive organs. When mature proglottids at the end of the tapeworm become distended with ova, they slough off the chain and are passed on the surface of the dog's stool. Segments are motile for a few minutes after they are passed.

A heavily infected dog often pass the moving proglottids directly from its anus. These segments are found on the hair around the dog's hindquarters, where they resemble dried grains of rice attached to the hair. These dried segments will eventually fall off the dog's hair into its bedding and serve as a source of food for flea larvae.

Tapeworms completely lack digestive organs in all stages of development. They absorb nutrients through their body walls from the liquid contents of the host's intestine and from the mucous membranes with which they come in contact. Mechanical obstruction of the intestines and the depletion of the host's nutrients are the most significant damages that tapeworms cause to their canine hosts.

D. caninum tapeworm segments have been seen passed on the stools of pups as young as six weeks of age. Since these parasites are acquired only through the ingestion of the intermediate host, the flea, infected puppies must have swallowed fleas when they were nursing from a flea-infested mother.

Nonprescription medications available for the treatment of tapeworms are very irritating to the host as well as to the worm, can be administered only after the dog has fasted, and will produce severe diarrhea and straining. A prescription drug is available, however, that can be administered either orally or by injection, is extremely safe and effective, and produces no irritation to the dog. Since this prescription drug is significantly superior to any OTC tapeworm medications, the use of the nonprescription products cannot be recommended. If you feel that you must try to treat your dog with a nonprescription medicine, the following OTC drugs are available.

Nonprescription Drugs for the Treatment of Hookworms and Tapeworms

CHEMICAL NAME OF DRUG	SOME BRAND NAMES	HOW SUPPLIED
Dichlorphene and toluene	TRIPLE WORMER	capsules
	TRI-WORMER	capsules
	TRIVERMICIDE	capsules
	ZEMA MULTIPURPOSE	capsules

Directions: Withhold food for at least 12 hours. Capsules must be swallowed whole to avoid irritation of mouth. Will produce severe purging.

Nonprescription Drugs for the Treatment of Tapeworms Only

CHEMICAL NAME OF DRUG	SOME BRAND NAMES	HOW SUPPLIED
Arecoline hydrobromide	WRM RID	powder

Directions: Withhold food for at least 12 hours. Do not treat pregnant, nursing, or debilitated animals. Will produce severe purging.

WHIPWORMS

The whipworm is a most aptly named parasite, as it resembles an old-fashioned stock whip with a thick, short handle and a long, coiled lash. The worms may be one-fourth inch or longer; the "head" is at the thin end, the reproductive organs in the thick end.

Trichuris vulpis, the canine whipworm, occupies the large intestine and the cecum of the dog. Ingestion of the embryonated eggs from contaminated environments will result in infestation.

Signs of whipworm may be mild or severe, depending on the extent of the dog's infestation. Intermittent diarrhea or stools that are partly liquid and partly formed, and weight loss accompanied by a ravenous appetite, may indicate a whipworm infection. Dogs infected with this parasite are usually adults or older puppies, since it takes the worms several weeks to reach maturity in the body of the dog. Only by finding the characteristic ova in the stool of the host can your veterinarian confirm a diagnosis of this parasite.

Most whipworm infections occur in the dog's cecum, a blind pouch of the intestinal tract that is analogous to the appendix of humans. As this site is almost inaccessible to most vermifuges, administering repeated doses of a prescription medication is the only effective method of eliminating this parasite. There are no nonprescription medications sold or recommended for the purpose.

13

JOINT, LIMB, AND LOCOMOTOR CONDITIONS

THE USE OF NONPRESCIPTION MEDICATIONS TO TREAT PAIN AND INFLAMMATION

Motion—walking, running, jumping, lying down, and getting up—is one of the most basic functions of a dog's life. The structures of the body that make motion possible form the *locomotor system.*

- *Bones* form the rigid framework of the body.
- *Joints* connect bones to other bones. Joints are composed of *cartilage, ligaments,* and *connective tissues.* Joints permit movement between adjacent bones.
- *Voluntary muscles* contract and relax to cause the limbs to move.
- *Tendons* attach muscles to the bones.
- *Nerves* relay impulses from the central nervous system to the muscles. Nerve impulses cause muscles to contract, thus producing voluntary movement of the parts of the body.

Lameness
When some part or all of these locomotor structures fail to function properly, the movement of the dog is impaired. *Lameness* or *limping* is the most common sign that one or

more of the structures of the locomotor system are not functioning correctly.

In most cases of lameness, structural problems cause the nerves to convey the sensation of pain to the dog's brain. It is this pain that causes the animal to limp. Only a few causes of lameness (such as paralysis) exist without the subject experiencing pain. The dog that carries a leg and walks on the other three is doing what comes naturally, sparing the injured limb and allowing time and rest to heal.

Lameness in dogs can be caused by many factors. Inherited abnormalities, developmental abnormalities, age-related structural changes, and injuries are among the most common.

Some of the conditions that produce lameness in dogs can benefit from the administration of nonprescription medication. Other conditions that cause lameness require surgery if the dog is ever to have normal movement. Still other conditions will respond to veterinary management without surgery. Some potential lameness-producing conditions can be handled by controlling the dog's diet, environment, or exercise. Many other conditions need no treatment at all—the dog will either recover from the condition or be able to function adequately in spite of the limp.

It is important to remember that a dog has four legs upon which to walk and run and that dogs with chronic lameness of a single limb or with one limb missing can function adequately with only three legs. Dogs with a missing or a chronically lame rear leg adjust to their handicap almost immediately; dogs that have problems with one front leg often require a little more time to get adjusted.

PROBLEMS OF YOUNG DOGS

Inherited abnormalities: genetically acquired from the parents
Inherited means "passed from the parents." *Congenital* means "present at birth." Not all congenital abnormalities

are inherited. A small percentage is caused by accidents in the uterus or mishaps during the birth process.

The presence of genes for an abnormality is not the only factor that controls the effect of the genes on the animal. Some puppies that inherit detrimental genes are lucky enough to be raised in an environment that minimizes the effect of these genes. Even though such puppies may grow into normal or nearly normal dogs, they should never be bred. They still possess the detrimental genes and will still pass the traits on to their offspring.

Puppies that inherit genes for limb abnormalities usually appear to be normal at birth. Their condition becomes apparent only later in life. Some inherited abnormalities may not show up until an affected dog is several years old and may already have been bred and passed the genes on to another generation.

HIP DYSPLASIA: THE MOST COMMON INHERITED LIMB ABNORMALITY OF DOGS

From the Greek words meaning "bad" *(dys)* and "formation" or "structure" *(plasia), dysplasia* indicates a badly

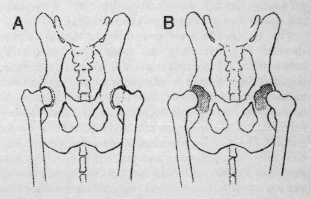

(A) Normal hips. (B) Hip dysplasia.

formed body part. *Hip dysplasia* (HD) means having badly formed hip *(coxofemural)* joints.

Hips are ball-and-socket joints. A hip joint consists of two main parts: the ball-shaped structure at the top of the femur (thighbone) and the bony socket of the pelvis into which this ball fits. In normal dogs, this ball is round and fits neatly and securely into the round socket of the pelvis, and the ligaments of the joint and musculature of the pelvic and thigh areas maintain correct joint alignment.

The configuration of the hip joint is governed by the bone structure of each individual breed. For example, the hips of a normal English bulldog are not exactly the same as the hips of a normal greyhound. Radiographically, the hip joints of all puppies will appear to be normal for their breed at birth. Joint abnormalities begin to develop only when the puppies begin to walk and run, thus bearing weight on their hip joints.

Hip dysplasia occurs in varying degrees of severity. The pup with mild hip dysplasia may appear to be normal or nearly normal, while the pup with moderate to severe hip dysplasia may get up slowly from a sitting position. It may have a swaying gait of the rear legs, be reluctant to jump, seem to tire easily, or cry out when it rises. Since hip dysplasia usually (but not always) affects both hips, a dysplastic dog will seldom be lame on only one hind leg.

Hip dysplasia is a common inherited trait in German shepherd dogs, retrievers, and many other large, heavy breeds of dog. The condition can also occur in mixed-breed dogs and dogs of small breeds. When puppies affected with hip dysplasia begin to walk, their muscles and ligaments do not hold the ball of their thighbone in the socket of their pelvis tightly, as do the muscles and ligaments of normal puppies. The resulting abnormal movement within the joint eventually causes damage and malformation of the joint structures. Puppies with mild dysplasia will appear to walk and run normally. More severely affected animals may have pain and abnormal gait at as young as four months of age.

The presence or absence of hip dysplasia and the degree to which any dog is affected can be determined with accuracy only by X rays of the pelvis. By observation only, even the most experienced veterinarian cannot detect with certainty whether a dog is free of the trait or how severely a dog is affected.

The *Orthopedic Foundation for Animals* (OFA) is a national organization that evaluates pelvic radiographs of dogs for the presence or absence of hip dysplasia. As the final conformation of a dog's hip joints can be determined only after the dog is mature, to be accepted for evaluation by the specialists at the OFA, the radiograph must be taken when the dog is two years of age or older.

A veterinarian in private practice will take the pelvic radiograph of an animal that the owners wish to have evaluated. These radiographs must conform to the OFA criteria for positioning of the subject. The veterinarian who has taken the X rays then submits the radiographs to the OFA. Three independent expert veterinary radiologists evaluate each film and assign the structure of each dog's hip joint one of seven classifications: *normal* (excellent, good, or fair) *borderline,* or *dysplastic* (mild, moderate, or severe.)

Hip dysplasia is *polygenetic;* the actions of several genes are involved in the presence and the severity of the condition. The only way to eliminate hip dysplasia from a breed is by not allowing any of the dogs that have genes for hip dysplasia to reproduce and perpetuate the trait. Conscientious breeders produce and sell puppies only from breeding stock that has hip radiographs evaluated as good or excellent by the OFA.

Minimize the chances that your dog will be affected with hip dysplasia

Nobody wants to purchase a puppy, only to discover later that the dog is crippled by severely dysplastic hips. Several precautions will help you have a sound dog.

1. If you are buying a new puppy, consider getting a breed with a low incidence of the condition.

2. Consider buying a dog of twelve months or older. By this age, the structure of the dog's hips will be close to the structure the hips will have when the dog is mature. A radiograph will therefore be likely to determine if the dog will be affected with HD, even though the dog is not old enough to have its pelvic radiographs submitted to the OFA.

3. If you buy a puppy of a breed that has a high incidence of hip dysplasia, insist that the puppy has *both* parents certified by the Orthopedic Foundation for Animals as having hips classified as excellent or good. Since hip dysplasia is a strongly inherited trait, puppies of dogs that have normal hips have a good chance of having normal hips themselves. To further improve the chances that your puppy will be normal, insist that all four of its grandparents, as well as both of its parents, were certified as normal by the OFA.

4. Keep all large-breed puppies thin. Fat puppies and puppies fed for maximum growth rate become so heavy that their excess body weight places extra stress on their hip joints. If these hip joints are compromised by the inheritance of hip dysplasia, heavy puppies will develop the condition more quickly and more severely than will thin puppies. Even large-breed puppies from stock thought to be free of inherited hip dysplasia should be kept lean until they are eighteen months to two years of age. In case any tendency to develop hip dysplasia is present in their genes, thin puppies' hip joints will be spared the burden of bearing excess weight.

Should the hips of every dog be X-rayed?
Must every dog of breeds in which HD is common be X-rayed for the presence or absence of hip dysplasia?

- *Yes* if the dog is ever intended to reproduce. No dog with any grade of HD other than excellent or good should ever be allowed to pass on its genes for this destructive trait.
- *Yes* if the dog displays any degree of hind-leg lameness or abnormal gait. A pelvic X ray will confirm or rule out HD as the cause of the dog's problems.
- *No* if the dog appears to be perfectly normal and is neutered or spayed. A X ray of a normal, nonreproductive dog is not harmful to the dog, but is not necessary for the dog's well-being. An X ray can always be taken later in the dog's life if the dog displays any hind-limb difficulty.

Managing the dysplastic dog

Any puppy or dog that is suspected of having hip dysplasia should be X-rayed and the radiograph evaluated by a competent veterinary radiologist. An X ray will rule out other possible causes of lameness or abnormal gait.

Dogs with severe hip dysplasia are often treated successfully with one of several surgical procedures; however, many dogs that have hip dysplasia do not require surgery. Unless the condition is severe, hip dysplasia often can be controlled in pet dogs by nonsurgical means:

• Keep the dysplastic dog lean throughout its entire life. Weight reduction, even in an old dog, often will produce a noticeable improvement your pet's ease of motion.

• Control the dysplastic dog's exercise. Dysplastic dogs need exercise, but they need slow and steady exercise to keep their muscles in tone without applying unnecessary stress to their deformed joints. Owners of dysplastic dogs should take them on long daily walks on a leash. It's good for man (or woman) and beast.

• Administer analgesics as needed. Many dysplastic dogs will need continuous medication, especially as they get older, to enable them to move in comfort. Steroids (cortisone) are often used for this purpose. Steroids are prescription drugs only, and can have detrimental side effects if given in high doses and/or for long periods of time.

Certain nonprescription human pain medications, the *nonsteroidal anti-inflammatory drugs* (NSAIDs) can be used to help the dysplastic dog live a more comfortable life. For more information on choosing an NSAID for your dog, see the section in Chapter 1 beginning on page 5.

—

Important:
NEVER *administer NSAIDs to cats*
without your veterinarian's approval.
Some NSAIDs are very toxic to cats

—

• Consider trying the newer drugs that enhance cartilage formation and maintenance through nutritional support. See listings under arthritis on page 184.

HYPERTROPHIC OSTEODYSTROPHY AND OSTEOCHONDROSIS

The term *hypertrophic osteodystrophy* (HOD) indicates bone growth in excess of normal. Affected puppies have swollen, painful joints, usually in the *metacarpal* (wrist) and *metatarsal* (hock) areas. The condition is most often seen in three- to six-month-old puppies, although a few puppies may be affected as late as ten months of age.

Osteochondrosis (OC) is a disease of growing cartilage cells. Pups with this condition commonly have pain and swelling in the shoulder, elbow, hock, and stifle (knee) joints.

HOD and OC are metabolic diseases that occur during periods of rapid bone growth. The tendency to have these conditions is inherited, but the *expression* of the condition is greatly influenced by environmental factors. This means that a puppy that inherits the genes for these diseases may not actually develop the conditions if its environment is favorable.

These diseases are not uncommon in large-breed puppies, and also can occur in medium-sized breeds. An affected puppy may have one or both of the conditions simultaneously or at different times during its period of fastest growth. Puppies usually "grow out of" hypertrophic osteodystrophy and osteochondrosis in a few months, though in some cases permanent joint damage remains throughout the dogs' lives.

There is strong evidence that the presence of these conditions is greatly influenced by the diet of growing puppies. Feeding tests conducted with young Great Danes have demonstrated that these conditions are about 75 percent preventable by proper management.

HOD and OC often are preventable conditions

• *Puppies should not be overfed.* Feeding a puppy too many calories will cause it to grow faster than is best for its health, and the puppy's bone formation will not be able to keep up with its growing body mass. Puppies that grow at an abnormally fast rate have an increased incidence of both osteochondrosis and hypertrophic osteodystrophy. A growing puppy, especially of the larger breeds, should never be fed as much as it will eat.

• *"Too much protein" is not a factor* in the development of these conditions. Dietary protein in excess of that which the body needs does not cause abnormalities of bone growth. A low-protein diet, however, may prevent the body from obtaining the amino acids it needs for optimum development.

• *The calcium and phosphorus content of pups' diets is critical to proper bone growth.* An incorrect amount and balance of calcium and phosphorus can cause bone and joint abnormalities. Too much or too little of either of these minerals is very detrimental to the health of the growing large-breed puppy.

Meat of any kind, including fish and chicken, should not be used as a supplement to a balanced diet of dog food. Meat is high in phosphorus, but low in calcium. The addition of significant amounts of meat, raw or cooked, to a puppy's diet will result in the puppy receiving an excess of phosphorus. When this excess is eliminated from the dog's body, it will carry with it some of the dog's dietary calcium. A dog fed a diet too rich in meat may become calcium-deficient and may suffer from bone abnormalities as a result.

Vitamin and mineral supplements, either human preparations or those intended for dogs, should not be added to a puppy's properly balanced diet. Dog food manufacturers gain their reputations by the performance of their products, and reputable dog food manufacturers include sufficient but not excessive quantities of these nutrients in their foods.

The safest, easiest, and least expensive way to feed a growing puppy correctly is to purchase a brand of dry dog food that contains necessary nutrients in the correct proportions. Feed your puppy this food exclusively and in the proper amounts. A food that contains 25 percent to 30 percent protein, approximately 0.8 percent calcium, and approximately 0.65 percent phosphorus is balanced for correct puppy nutrition.

"Puppy food" formulated for large breeds may be restricted in caloric density to enable the owner to feed the puppy a larger volume of food and still keep it in lean condition. Feeding the puppy a higher-calorie food in smaller amounts will produce the same effect. The adult size of a dog is determined by its genetic makeup, but the large puppy that is fed fewer calories a day during its growing period will take a little longer to reach its final size. This slightly slower growth rate will aid the proper formation of its bones.

UNUNITED ANCONEAL PROCESS (ELBOW DYSPLASIA)

The bones of the forearm are the *radius* and the *ulna*. The *humerus,* the bone of the upper arm, fits into a semicircular notch at the top of the ulna. A projection of the ulna, the *olecranon,* makes up the point of the elbow.

The upper edge of the notch into which the humerus fits is composed of the *anconeal process.* This small piece of bone is formed separately from the main body of the ulna and fuses with the ulna shortly after the puppy's birth. If these pieces of bone do not fuse, the loose anconeal process will cause pain and damage to the elbow joint.

The only treatment that will restore pain-free motion to the affected dog's front leg is surgery to remove the offending bone fragment. Analgesic drugs are of little help as long as the loose piece of bone remains in the dog's elbow.

The Orthopedic Foundation for Animals evaluates radiographs of the elbow joints as well as hip joints. If you are considering the purchase of a puppy of a large or giant breed in which ununited anconeal process is common, ask to see the parents' OFA certificate for the absence of this trait.

CONGENITAL LUXATED PATELLA ("SLIPPED STIFLE" OR DISPLACED KNEECAP)

The *stifle* is the joint of the hind leg between the *femur* (thighbone) and the *tibia* (shinbone.) The *stifle joint* of the dog corresponds to the *knee joint* of the human.

The *patella,* the kneecap, is a small, rounded bone normally located at the front of the stifle. The patella is held in position by ligaments and by the bony structure of the joint itself. When the patella is not in the correct position, it is said to be *luxated.*

Congenital malformations of the bones of the stifle may cause the patella to be displaced from its correct position at the front of the joint, usually to an abnormal *medial* position

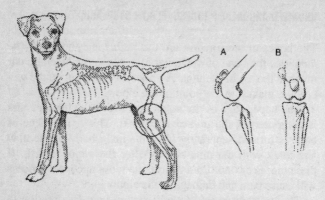

"Slipped stifle." The kneecap is displaced upward and toward the inside of the leg. (A) Side view. (B) Front view.

toward the inner surface of the joint. Some of these displacements are intermittent; some are permanent. The condition can occur in several degrees of severity. Breeders know these conditions as "slipped stifle."

Malformations that result in permanently luxated patellae are commonly inherited in some of the small and toy breeds of dogs. The hind legs of the puppies that inherit this condition are normal at birth, but the structures that should hold the patellae in place are not properly formed. When the puppies begin to walk, their kneecaps slip toward the inside of their stifle joints. The patellae of dogs with this condition remain in the abnormal medially luxated position. In many cases, both legs are affected equally. Puppies with this condition learn to walk and run on these malformed joints. Although their gait may be abnormal and they may have a bowlegged appearance, the condition is painless to the young dog and usually needs no treatment. As dogs with slipped stifles get older, however, they may suffer from arthritic problems in their stifles.

Many of the dogs affected with congenital permanently luxated patellae are long-haired, short-legged toy breeds such as the Pekingese, the Lhasa apso, and the Shih Tzu. The profuse coats of these breeds may mask the condition to all but the most careful observers. In heavily coated breeds, luxuated patellae can be detected by palpation (feeling) by veterinarians, dog-show judges, and knowledgeable breeders.

Some small and toy breed dogs may inherit a degree of slipped stifle that is not the same as those with permanent luxations. These dogs are born with joints in which the patella is not stable and can slip in and out of its correct position. In these dogs the patella does not remain fixed in the abnormal position. This condition is intermittent but may become permanent. Often one leg is affected more severely than the other. Dogs with an intermittent slipped stifle will often walk on three legs and carry the painful leg in a flexed position.

Joint surgery may be used to correct intermittent luxated patellae, but since the condition is inherited, all dogs with this trait should be neutered, so that the condition will not be passed to the next generation.

The administration of NSAIDs as painkillers or anti-inflammatory agents is seldom indicated, as these drugs have only a temporary effect. The drugs may reduce the pain, but they will not cause the patella to become more stable. Surgery is the only effective treatment for the condition.

Congenital Structural Defects of Dogs Associated with Lameness

CONDITION	STRUCTURE AFFECTED	AGE AT ONSET	BREED OR SIZE	METHOD OF DIAGNOSIS
Hip dysplasia	hip joints	4 months to 2 years	large breeds	radiographs
Elbow dysplasia	elbow joints	4–6 months	medium & large	radiographs
Luxated patella	stifles (knees)	2 months or older	small & toy	palpation

**Congenital Structural Defects
of Dogs Associated with Lameness (continued)**

CONDITION	STRUCTURE AFFECTED	AGE AT ONSET	BREED OR SIZE	METHOD OF DIAGNOSIS
Osteo-chondrosis	leg joints	3–6 months	large & giant	signs & radiographs
Hypertrophic osteo-dystrophy	leg joints	3–10 months	large & giant	signs & radiographs

"SWIMMER" PUPPIES

Although "swimmer" puppies have been seen and treated by veterinarians and dog breeders for decades, this is not a common condition. Swimmers can appear in all breeds of dogs, from toy to giant breeds. A swimmer is usually a member of a very small litter, or occasionally it is the only puppy in a litter. The swimmer is usually bigger, fatter, and better looking than the other puppies. It does not stand and walk when its littermates do; instead, the swimmer lies on its stomach with each back leg extended out to the side. The term *swimmer* originates from the frog-swimming position of the pup's hind legs.

The swimmer propels itself forward by pulling itself along with its front legs, and continues to receive its share of mother's milk. When the pups are offered food, the swimmer manages to reach the dish and eat. The swimmer uses its front legs normally; only the hind legs are affected. The swimmer is unable to support its body weight on its hind legs.

Often a swimmer will still be "swimming" when its littermates are scampering about in their enclosure. Swimmer

puppies are not suffering from joint deformity, from vitamin-mineral imbalance, or from being crushed by the
mother. They are simply too heavy. Their weight exceeds the
ability of their immature legs to get beneath their bodies to
support them.

Some swimmers need only a rough surface to get their
legs under them. If the swimmer puppy is placed on a rough
surface such as carpet, it may be better able to obtain traction with its hind feet than it can when placed on a smooth
surface such as newspapers. Knowledgeable breeders often
place a piece of old carpeting in the puppies' box to help
heavy puppies learn to walk.

Many puppies are temporary swimmers. Even without
treatment, most puppies that are swimmers do not "swim"
for very long. They learn to walk only a few days to a week
later than their littermates. Temporary swimmers seldom receive veterinary attention for their problem, since they become "normal" within a few days. A busy veterinary practice
will see a true swimmer puppy only once or twice a year.

—

*A puppy that has been walking, but suddenly becomes a
"swimmer," may have sustained an injury. It should be examined
by a veterinarian immediately.*

—

Puppies should be helped if they do not support their
weight on their hind legs by twenty-eight to thirty days of
age. Though it is likely that swimmer puppies will eventually walk normally without treatment, as the treatment is so
easily accomplished, delay is unnecessary.

To "cure" a swimmer you need only a roll of adhesive
tape (½ inch wide for very small breed puppies, ¾ or 1 inch
for larger ones). The hind legs of the pup are taped in such a
manner that it is impossible for both legs to spread to the
sides at the same time. When the tape is applied correctly,
the puppy will be forced to lie with both hind legs to the left

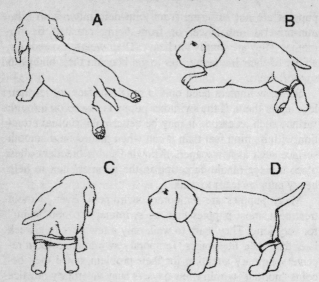

A "swimmer" puppy. (A) The puppy is too heavy to get his hind legs together under its body. (B) The legs are taped together just above the hocks. (C) The puppy's legs cannot spread to each side, and it can stand. (D) Within minutes the puppy can walk almost normally.

or both hind legs to the right. From this position, the puppy will be able to get both hind legs under its body at once. It will stand and walk almost immediately.

Here is how to tape the legs of a swimmer:

1. Tear off about a 10-inch strip of tape for a two-pound puppy. Use a longer strip for a larger pup, a shorter strip for a smaller one.

2. Wrap one end of the tape around one of the pup's hind legs just above the hock. Stick the tape firmly onto the hair, but do not apply it tightly enough to cut off circulation or to

inhibit normal movements of the tendons. More than one wrap of the tape may be needed.

3. Bring the free end of the strip of tape to the other hind leg. Calculate the normal distance between the hind legs if the puppy were standing. Wrap the tape around the other hind leg above the hock, leaving a strip of tape joining the two hind legs equal in length to the normal distance between the standing pups' hind legs. The tape joining the two hind legs should be long enough for the pup to take a normal-length step. If in doubt as to distance, make the length of the tape joining the legs too long rather than too short.

4. Stick the free end of the tape back along the original piece between the pup's legs. This piece of tape will now be doubled, sticky side in.

5. Place the puppy on the ground. Because of the tape between its legs, it will be unable to lie flat on its belly with a leg to each side and will be forced to lie with both hind legs to the right or with both hind legs to the left. From either of these positions, the puppy will be able to scramble both hind legs under its body and stand up. Swimmers often stand and walk within minutes of having the tape applied.

6. Leave the tape in place for two weeks to allow the puppy's legs to get strong. If the tape loosens on the legs, apply new tape. If the tape strip between the legs appears to be too short as the puppy grows, cut the strip and lengthen it with a new piece of tape. After two weeks, remove the tape but observe the puppy. If it lies in the "swimming" position more than occasionally, apply new tape and leave it on for two more weeks. Very few former swimmers will need their legs taped for a second two weeks.

PROBLEMS RELATED TO AGE OR INJURY

Degenerative arthritis (osteoarthritis)

Ouch! It happens to all of us as we get older, and it happens to our aging dogs as well. The joint cartilage wears out. Inflammatory changes in the bony structures of the joints cause pain, swelling, and immobility. The term that is commonly used for this degenerative joint disease is *arthritis.*

The degeneration of joints in aging dogs is the most common cause, but not the only cause, of arthritis. Hip dysplasia and traumatic injury to joints can result in arthritis in dogs of any age. Whenever a joint is damaged badly enough to create permanent changes, arthritis is the result.

Locomotor Problems Associated with Age

CONDITION	AFFECTED PART	AGE AT ONSET	BREED OR SIZE	METHOD OF DIAGNOSIS
Osteoarthritis	all joints	middle & old age	all breeds	signs & radiographs
Intervertebral disc disease	spine	middle & old age	all breeds	signs & radiographs
Osteosarcoma (bone cancer)	long bones	middle & old age	mainly large breeds	radiographs

Just as in obese and inactive humans, degenerative arthritis often occurs earlier in the life of obese and inactive dogs. Thin dogs, active dogs, and dogs of the small and medium breeds often show no arthritic signs until they are of an advanced age.

Dogs' arthritic signs are the same as humans: stiffness, joint pain, sometimes joint swelling, and heat in the joints.

Dogs' early arthritic signs often ease after the patients are in motion, only to return after a period of inactivity. This is called "warming out" of the condition. As arthritis progresses, the warming-out period will become longer and less complete. Eventually pain will cause the dog to try to move the affected joints as little as possible.

An owner may treat his dog's degenerative arthritis as he might treat his own. In mild cases, the human sufferer will take aspirin or other NSAIDs for pain as needed. An owner can safely administer most of the same drugs, in appropriate doses, to an arthritic dog. Just as a human arthritis sufferer may then make an appointment with a doctor if she gets little or no relief from OTC drugs, so should an appointment be made with a veterinarian if the dog's pain is not sufficiently eased by OTC treatment. Your vet can perform diagnostic tests such as radiographs to confirm or exclude the presence of degenerative arthritis. If the diagnosis is confirmed, the veterinarian will recommend appropriate analgesics that may be OTC drugs or may be prescription drugs such as cortisone.

Suspect degenerative arthritis when these factors are present:

• The dog is elderly for its breed. Aging is strongly related to the dog's breed and type. Smaller breeds are not really old until they are twelve or fourteen; giant breeds may be quite old at seven or eight years. "Old" for a fox terrier is not the same as "old" for a Great Dane.

• The dog's signs of stiffness and pain have gradually become apparent. Arthritis is a condition that does not appear suddenly.

• The condition is most apparent after the dog has been at rest. Many elderly dogs (and humans) get up stiff and sore, but "warm out of it" as the day progresses.

• The condition becomes worse after unaccustomed strenuous exercise. For example, an old retriever is fine until the
day after the hunting season opens. The dog then appears to
be just as stiff and sore as is its sedentary old owner after a
day of walking through fields or sitting in a frigid duck blind.

• The dog is otherwise normal. It eats and drinks as usual.
Its bowel and bladder habits have not changed.

• The condition *does not* involve just a single limb. A dog
that favors one leg has an abnormality of that limb, not generalized degenerative arthritis.

• The dog improves after properly administered analgesics
or drugs that enhance cartilage formation.

Every owner must subjectively evaluate his dog's signs.
The better the owner understands what is "normal" for his
dog, the more able he will be to tell if the dog is abnormal.

Nutritional supplements to promote cartilage health

Some preparations designed to contribute to the health of
joint cartilage and ease the effects of arthritis are considered
to be nutrients rather than drugs. The generic names of these
"chondroprotective" agents are *glucosamine* and *chron-
doitin*. It is believed that glucosamine stimulates the metabolism of cartilage cells and that chondroitin inhibits the
enzymes that break down these cells.

Glucosamine is given alone or in combination with chondroitin. The intent of these products is to maintain and restore
the health of joint cartilage and thereby relieve the signs of osteoarthritis. A human or animal must receive the preparation
for four to six weeks before maximum results will be seen.

Glucosamine and chondroitin are available as nonprescription preparations for humans, dogs, cats, and horses. Except
for the size of the dose, the products are essentially the same.

Nonprescription Nutrients for Promotion of Joint Health

ACTIVE INGREDIENTS	HOW SUPPLIED
Glucosamine HCl & sulfate	500-mg tablets for humans and dogs
Chondroitin sulfate with glucosamine HCl & sulfate	400 mg chondroitin with 500 mg of glucosamine
(for toy breeds)	100 mg of chondroitin with 124 mg of glucosamine

—

Signs that an owner may regard as arthritis can indicate other conditions. If a dog gets no better after a short course of treatment with an NSAID, the owner should make a veterinary appointment without delay.

—

Disease of the spine

The spinal column is composed of individual bones, the vertebrae. Most dogs have seven *cervical* (neck), thirteen *thoracic* (chest), seven *lumbar* (lower back,) and three *sacral* (pelvic) vertebrae. The average dog is also born with between twenty and twenty-five *coccygeal* (tail) vertebrae. Dogs born with bob tails or screw tails have fewer coccygeal vertebrae; these vertebrae are often malformed.

The bones of the spine form a hollow protective tube for the spinal cord. The lower surfaces at which the bony vertebrae contact each other are padded with discs of fibrous material, *intervertebral discs*. The intervertebral discs and the spaces between the vertebrae form joints that allow the spine to be flexible.

All abnormal conditions of the vertebrae are serious, because the spinal cord is enclosed within the vertebral column. Damage to the vertebrae often results in damage to the spinal cord. An animal with a damaged spinal cord may suffer partial or complete loss of control of its body functions, up to and including paralysis and death.

Intervertebral disc disease: A common disease of the spine in dogs is *intervertebral disc disease*. This condition occurs when the fibrous intervertebral discs between the vertebrae prolapse into the space occupied by the spinal cord. Signs of disc disease often appear suddenly. The condition is most common in long-backed, short-legged breeds such as the dachshund. While displaced intervertebral discs in humans usually cause only pain, because of the difference in the anatomy of the human and canine spinal cord, in dogs prolapsed discs may cause partial or complete paralysis of the patient's hindquarters.

Spondylitis and spondylosis: These terms refer to inflammation and subsequent new abnormal bone formation at the joints between the vertebrae.

Signs: The signs of these diseases are caused by the interruption of the normal nerve function of the spinal cord. A dog with spondylitis or spondylosis may be wobbly, or instable in its rear quarters. It may drag its hind feet, a condition known as "knuckling." If the motor neurons that control bladder and bowel function are damaged, a dog with a disease of the spine may have fecal or urinary incontinence, constipation, or inability to urinate. Dogs affected with spinal disease are usually of middle age or older. Some spinal disease is caused by hereditary deformity of the vertebrae; some is caused by degenerative changes.

—

Surgery is the only treatment that may be successful for diseases of the spine. The use of nonprescription drugs for these conditions is not effective and is never recommended.

—

Osteosarcoma (cancer of the bone)

Osteo refers to bone, *sarcoma* to a malignant tumor. The common name for this condition is *cancer of the bone*. Bone cancer is diagnosed primarily by X ray, and occasionally by bone biopsy.

Malignant tumors of bones are most common in middle-aged to old dogs of the larger breeds. These tumors appear most frequently (but not exclusively) in the upper bones of the front and hind legs. If an osteosarcoma is diagnosed before the tumor has spread to the patient's internal organs, the condition may be treated successfully by chemotherapy and/or amputation of the affected limb. Almost every dog accepts an amputation with no difficulty; almost every owner accepts a dog with an amputation once the sutures are removed and the hair grows back over the operative site. No owner should hesitate to have his dog undergo an amputation if that is the only way to save the dog's life.

The earlier in the course of the disease that the diagnosis of osteosarcoma is made, the better the chances are for successful treatment. If the tumor has spread to the lungs or other organs, surgery is not likely to prolong the life of the patient.

Early signs of bone cancer resemble signs of many other, less serious conditions.

Suspect osteosarcoma when these conditions are present:

- The dog is middle-aged to old, of a large breed.
- There is no history of trauma to the dog's limb, nor is there any evidence of a wound.
- The dog's lameness is always in the same limb.
- The lameness gradually gets worse over a period of days or weeks.
- The lameness never entirely disappears, even when analgesics are administered.

Obviously, bone cancer cannot be treated with nonprescription drugs, and seldom can be treated successfully without surgical or chemotherapeutic procedures. If a large older dog is lame in one leg without apparent cause and if the lameness does not improve within a few days, diagnostic radiographs should be taken to detect or eliminate a diagnosis of osteosarcoma.

Fractures of the Bones of the Limbs

Being hit by a car is the most common cause of severe injury to dogs. This is an almost entirely preventable situation. If no dogs ran loose without adequate supervision to ensure their safety, fewer owners would be faced with the loss of their pets or with large veterinary bills.

The primary cause of fractures of the leg is severe trauma and/or unusual twisting force. In a *simple fracture,* the skin is unbroken. In a *compound fracture,* the skin is broken and pieces of the bone may protrude through the wound.

Fractures are described by the way in which the bone is damaged

---

TYPES OF FRACTURES

- *Oblique fractures* are very common. In these fractures, the bones are broken on an angle. The pieces may or may not remain in alignment.
- *Transverse fractures* are those in which the bone is broken straight through both sides.
- *Spiral fractures* may result when bones are twisted at the time the fractures occur.
- *Greenstick fractures* are those in which the bone is not broken clear through both sides. The pieces of a bone with a greenstick fracture remain in normal alignment.

- *Comminuted fractures* are those in which the bones are broken into three or more pieces.

Signs of a fractured leg

- Fractures are very painful to the victim. A dog with a fracture will refuse to bear weight on the affected leg, will resist handling of the leg, and may cry out in pain when the leg is moved.

- A fractured leg may appear to be deformed. The leg may swing or flop in an abnormal manner. Swelling is often present within minutes of the occurrence of a fracture.

- In a compound fracture, the skin is broken and ends of the bone may be visible in the wound.

- *Crepitation* (the feel or sound of broken ends of bone grinding together) may be present.

The diagnosis of a fracture and the assessment of the severity of the condition ordinarily require a radiograph. Po-

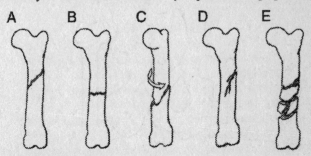

Types of fractures. (A) Oblique. (B) Transverse. (C) Spiral. (D) Greenstick. (E) Comminuted.

sitioning an injured dog for a radiograph is painful and should be done under sedation or anesthesia.

EVERY fracture of a limb bone requires prompt veterinary care. The victim should be transported with as little additional trauma to the injured limb as possible. Owners should not attempt to apply splints or other devices to limbs suspected of being fractured—such treatment often results in making a bad situation worse. For more information on transporting an injured dog, see page 18.

Fractures of the pelvis (hip) and scapula (shoulder)

Immediately after the trauma, a dog that has suffered a broken pelvis or scapula will be severely lame on the leg on the affected side. The leg itself may not appear to be damaged, but the dog will be unable to use the limb and will be in significant pain. These injuries should be handled exactly as are fractured bones of the leg: the victim should be taken to a veterinary hospital without delay.

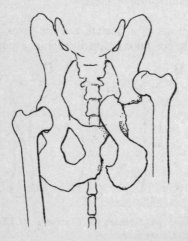

Fractured pelvis.

Fractures of the skull and spine

These are among the most serious injuries that a dog can suffer. Fractures involving the head may result in bleeding inside of the skull and death. Fractures of the spine that are accompanied by significant displacement of the vertebrae will often result in complete and irreversible paralysis of the hindquarters or even of the entire body of the victim.

Any dog suspected of suffering from fractures of the head and spine must be transported to the nearest veterinary facility in such a way as to prevent additional damage. A blanket or a coat that is held by two people at the corners can be used to improvise a stretcher.

Joint dislocation and ligament rupture

It is often impossible to tell without an X ray if an injury is a broken bone, a ruptured ligament, or a dislocated joint. Often (but not always) the pain of ligament rupture or joint dislocation is not as severe as the pain of a fracture. Often these injuries are not as swollen or deformed in appearance as are fractures. However, if a dog remains severely or even moderately lame three or four hours after suffering trauma, a visit to your veterinarian is in order. Nonprescription analgesic drugs may reduce the pain of ligament tears and dislocations, but these drugs will not contribute in any way to repairing the injury. If a dog with a dislocation is neglected for more than twenty-four hours, it may be difficult or impossible to restore normal function to the damaged part without extensive (and expensive) surgery.

Sprains, strains, and bruises

All of these conditions are caused by trauma. Even if the damage is relatively minor, the dog usually will show evidence of pain.

The difference between a sprain and a strain is one of degree. A sprain is significant damage short of complete tear-ing of the ligaments of a joint, while a strain is minor damage to a ligament caused by abnormal stretching or twisting.

A bruise is bleeding within a muscle or under the skin, caused by blunt trauma that does not break the skin, but that does damage to the small blood vessels, allowing blood to seep into the tissues. The presence of pain depends on the location and severity of the bruise. Bruised areas may not be painful unless they are touched. On humans, bruises are "black and blue" spots, but on dogs the discoloration can be difficult to see. Color change may be apparent only on white or light-colored dogs and only when the hair is parted.

Signs of a sprain, strain, or bruise:

• In most cases, the patient has suffered an observed injury. It might have jumped off a bed, fallen down the stairs, or even been bumped by a slow-moving car.

• The dog with a sprain or strain will probably have cried out at the time of the injury, but will not continue to vocalize for more than a few minutes. The dog with a sprain or a strain will not cry out every time it tries to move.

• The dog may limp significantly or carry the injured limb, but will not be reluctant to move, nor will it resent gentle handling of the limb.

• A sprained or strained limb is not abnormal in shape or position, nor does the leg swing or move in an unusual way. Just as with a human sprain, a dog's sprain may show swelling, heat, and redness, but these characteristics can be difficult to detect under the coat.

Human sprains and strains are traditionally treated with *"RICE": rest, ice, compression, and elevation.* Dogs will rest their own sprains by favoring the leg, but will usually resist the remainder of human therapy. Dogs dislike the application to ice to their injuries, will usually chew off compression bandages, and will refuse to lie with the injured limb in an elevated position. If you are sure that the dog has suffered nothing more serious than a sprain, strain, or bruise, restrict its exercise and relieve its pain with analgesics until the injury is no longer painful. The length of time required for sprains and strains to heal averages one to three weeks, depending on the severity of the injury. Pain-relieving medications should be needed for only a few days.

Fracture of toes, rupture of tendons of toes

Metacarpal and *metatarsal* bones correspond to the bones of the back of a human hand and the arch of a human foot. *Phalanxes* are the small bones of the digits (fingers and toes). If one or more of the metacarpal or metatarsal bones are broken in a dog's foot, a veterinarian should see the victim. These fractures require casting or surgery just as do fractures of the long bones of the limbs.

Dogs occasionally sustain trauma to their feet that causes fractures of one or more of the phalanxes. The most common source of this trauma is being accidentally stepped on by a human, and the second common cause is being struck on the foot by a falling object.

The dog with a fracture of a toe bone will usually exhibit mild to moderate lameness and will cry out if the digit is touched. Just as with a human broken toe, a dog's injured digit is often swollen—and just as with a human broken toe, surgery or the application of a splint is seldom necessary unless gross displacement of the fragments has occurred.

If gross displacement of the bones or a compound fracture is not present, dogs often do best if the fracture is allowed to heal without treatment. If the dog seems to have much pain, analgesics can be given. If the fragments of a dog's broken toe *must* be immobilized, a whole-foot cast should be applied over the splint; dogs will invariable chew off a splint applied alone to a toe. Splinting or casting of digits suspected of being fractured is a job for a veterinarian. Devices applied by an owner often do more harm than good. When in doubt, leave it alone!

"Flat" toes—rupture or displacement of the tendons of the toe

Injuries to the flexor tendons of the dog's foot can occur when an animal is running and obtaining maximum traction on rough surfaces. Racing and hunting dogs are at increased risk for this type of tendon injury.

If a flexor tendon of a digit is ruptured or torn loose, the toe no longer is maintained in its normal arched position. Instead of the toe being flexed with the toenail touching the ground, the bones of the toe are in a straight line, the toe is flat, and the nail sticks up. This injury appears to be entirely painless to the dog; the owner will simply notice that the dog now has one or more flat toes, when yesterday the foot appeared to be normal.

"Flat" toes are neither painful nor disabling to a dog. Unless several toes of any one foot are affected, rupture of the tendons of the toe is almost entirely a cosmetic injury even on racing and hunting dogs. When flat toes occur on a show dog, the defect is so obviously acquired as to be disregarded by any knowledgeable judge.

Surgery is the only corrective measure for ruptured tendons of the toes. As previously mentioned, flat toes are not debilitating to the dog, so surgery is merely of cosmetic value. To have any chance for success, the surgery must be performed within twelve hours of the injury. After a few hours, irreversible changes occur at the ruptured ends of the tendons, making the repair difficult and success doubtful.

Since the nail of a flat toe no longer touches the ground, it will not be subject to normal wear and will soon become overgrown. Owners of dogs with flat toes must remember to trim the nail on the affected digit—otherwise, this condition needs no treatment.

Broken toenails

Each of the four weight-bearing digits (toes) of a dog's foot is made up of three bones, the first, the second, and third *phalanxes*. The terminal phalanx, or last bone of each toe, bears a projection of bone around which the nail grows. The cavity between the bony projection and the nail is filled with a pulp of tissue, blood vessels, and nerves.

The bony core of the dog's nail remains the same size throughout the dog's adult life. As a dog's toenail grows, the nerve and blood vessel in the pulp cavity between the nail and the bone also grow, although these structures will never extend to the tip of the nail. If a dog's nails are allowed to become excessively long, the nails cannot be cut back to their original length without cutting into the pulp cavity. If the nerve and blood vessel of the pulp cavity are cut when a dog's nail is trimmed, it will cause pain and bleeding.

Overgrown nails tend to break. If only the dead end of the nail is broken, neither pain nor bleeding will be caused. The most common injury to a dog's overgrown toenail, however, is an incomplete fracture at the point at which the nail emerges from the skin of the toe. This fracture damages functioning nerves and blood vessels, and though any bleeding will stop after a few minutes, the injured nerve will continue to transmit pain impulses whenever pressure is exerted on the broken nail. Because of this pain, the relatively minor injury of a broken toenail can cause a dog to become surprisingly lame.

Diagnosis of a broken nail: Often the existence of a broken toenail is obvious: the dog favors one foot and vigorously resists any handling of the foot. Upon examination a nail is discovered to be broken or missing. Some broken nails bleed, and some do not, depending on the site of the fracture. If bleeding occurs with a broken toenail, it can be stopped by the application of styptic powder or a styptic pencil held firmly on the area. In the absence of styptic products, a pinch of table sugar pressed to the bleeding surface will promote coagulation.

If a nail is broken at the junction of the nail and the skin (the nail bed) but the broken part of the nail remains held in place by a bit of the surrounding tissue, the cause of the dog's pain might not be obvious. The broken nail will look like all the others. However, the broken nail will move freely when manipulated (and the dog will yelp). Unbroken nails will feel firmly attached to the underlying bony structure. Manipulation of these nails will not cause pain.

Treatment of a broken toenail: If the nail is broken at any point, the movement of the loose fragment is the cause of the dog's pain. Obviously, the first course of action is to remove the fragment.

If the nail fragment is connected only by a bit of tissue, it may be possible to yank the fragment off before the dog realizes what is happening. If the fragment is connected by a large amount of undamaged tissue, it will be necessary to

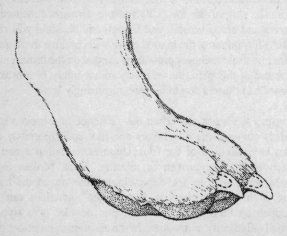

Anatomy of a toenail.

trim the broken part away using a *sharp* guillotine-type dog nail-trimming tool. Trimming a broken nail may cause the dog momentary pain; the handler must take care to avoid being bitten (see illustration on page 200).

If the nail is broken at the nail bed, the fragment cannot be trimmed off in its entirety, as the bony core of the nail is inside the fragment. In such a case, the nail should be shortened as much as possible without cutting into the blood supply. This will prevent the fragment from touching the ground when the dog walks and minimize the pain the dog experiences. Some nails broken at the nail bed will heal; some will fall off entirely, but in either case, the dog will almost invariably grow a new nail.

Expect a dog with a broken nail to lick its foot and keep the area free of debris. Antibiotics are rarely needed to prevent infection at the site of a broken nail. Bandaging a broken nail is almost never indicated. It is difficult to keep a bandaged foot dry; a wet bandage is nothing but a breeding ground for infectious organisms.

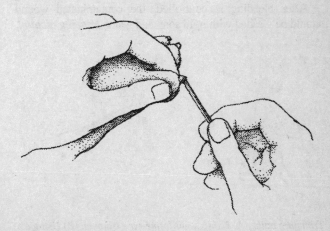

Applying styptic to a bleeding nail.

Prevent broken nails: Nails that are kept at a reasonable length are seldom broken. A dog could break even a short nail if it catches it on something and jerks its foot away, but almost all broken nails are the result of the nail being allowed to become overgrown.

Laceration of footpads

The large *metacarpal pad* and the four smaller *digital pads* on the bottom of a dog's foot are easily lacerated when a dog steps on broken glass, discarded metal, or other trash in its environment. Unfortunately, there are increasingly few places in which an owner can exercise his dog that are free of such debris.

Diagnosis of an injured footpad is easy: the dog suddenly is lame and the injury often bleeds. Treatment of footpad injuries depends upon the severity of each case.

Cut footpads often bleed profusely, requiring a pressure bandage to control the hemorrhage (see page 88). It is extremely important that the pressure bandage is removed after a maximum of two hours; if bleeding persists, the bandage can always be reapplied.

After bleeding is controlled, the contaminated wound should be washed with mild soap and water. ***Pouring alcohol,***

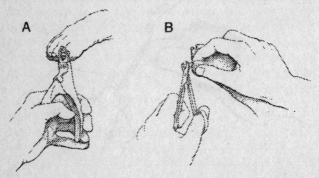

Trimming nails. (A) Using a guillotine-type trimmer. (B) Using a scissors-type trimmer.

Merthiolate, or iodine into the wound is absolutely contraindicated. Not only is such treatment painful to the dog, but such medications delay the formation of healthy granulation tissue by destroying new cells that are growing into the wound.

The injured dog should be kept in a relatively clean, dry environment for a day or two, until new granulation tissue begins to fill the wound. As with most other injuries of dogs' feet, bandaging a cut paw is usually not indicated. Even if antibiotic cream is applied, the damp environment inside a bandage promotes bacterial growth. If a bandage must be applied, it must be removed and the foot thoroughly cleaned before a new bandage is replaced. This must be done at a minimum of every twelve hours.

The footpads of a dog consist of hairless, black, dense, keratinized epithelium. This tissue seldom heals by first intention no matter what treatment is instituted. Even if the injured dog is anesthetized and the wound is sutured immediately, the edges of the cut usually do not heal together. Instead, new granulation tissue will grow to fill the wound. Initially the healing pad will have a wedge of pink tissue at the site of the injury. Within a few weeks the tissue will become keratinized and appear almost exactly as it did before it was cut.

An appropriate way to prevent infection in a cut footpad is to spray or dust the area with wound powder every eight to twelve hours. The dog should be prevented from licking its injury for twenty minutes after each application of the powder; this will allow the medication time to kill bacteria on the surface of the wound.

Sudden Causes of Lameness

CONDITION	SIGNS	TREATMENT
Fractures of the bones of the limbs	Severe pain, deformity, and/or crepitation	*Emergency!* Rush to veterinarian

Sudden Causes of Lameness (*continued*)

CONDITION	SIGNS	TREATMENT
Fractures of the pelvis and scapula	Inability to use limb	*Emergency!* Rush to veterinarian
Fractures of the skull and spine	Loss of consciousness, complete or partial paralysis	*Emergency!* Rush to veterinarian
Ligament rupture or joint dislocation	Lameness with or without limb deformity	Veterinary care within 12 hours
Sprains, strains, and bruises	Mild to moderate lameness	Rest, analgesics
Fracture of toes, ruptured tendons of toes	No lameness to moderate lameness	No treatment (surgery optional)
Broken toenails	Limping, bleeding nail	Remove broken part, use blood coagulant
Laceration of footpads	Lameness, bleeding	Stop bleeding, apply antiseptic powder

14

THE HEART AND LUNGS

In dogs, as in all other mammals, the heart is a four-chambered, two-stage pump. Oxygen-depleted blood enters the heart and is moved to the lungs, where the red blood cells take up oxygen. The oxygenated blood is then moved back to the heart, where it is pumped throughout the body. If the heart cannot move an adequate volume of blood or if the lungs cannot supply an adequate amount of oxygen, the dog will suffer tissue damage, shortness of breath, and possibly death.

Many conditions can cause heart problems. Congenital defects of the heart and circulatory system; tumors of the heart or lungs; and bacterial, viral, or fungal disease are only a few. *Dilated cardiomyopathy,* a condition in which the heart muscles are thickened and weakened, is thought to be an inherited trait in the Doberman pinscher and other breeds of dogs. Heartworm infection can affect any dog or cat.

Because the life of every animal depends on the adequate function of the heart and lungs, any condition that adversely affects these organs is potentially fatal. Only a qualified veterinarian, therefore, can treat these conditions. If you suspect a circulatory condition, see your veterinarian immediately. Dogs in which heart or lung disease is recognized in the early stages are more likely to respond to treatment than are dogs that are very sick before therapy is begun.

CONGESTIVE HEART FAILURE

The term *heart failure* describes a heart that is failing to pump an adequate amount of blood throughout the body. *Congestive heart failure* is when, as a result of insufficient blood circulation, fluid accumulates in the lungs. In severe conditions, fluid may also accumulate in the tissues, usually in the legs.

The signs of congestive heart failure usually appear in middle-aged or older dogs. These signs include shortness of breath, difficulty breathing *(dyspnea)*, blue or gray mucous membranes of the lips and gums *(cyanosis)* exercise intolerance, swelling of the limbs *(edema)*, and cardiac cough.

The first sign often shown by an older dog with a heart condition is a cough at night when the dog is inactive. In the early stages of the disease this cough will disappear during the day when the dog moves around, but eventually the dog will cough all the time and will cough violently if forced to exercise.

Congestive heart failure in dogs may be caused by a disease of the heart muscle, a defect of the heart valves, or a mechanical obstruction of the heart and major vessels such as occurs in heartworm infection. The same drugs and procedures for treating human cardiac patients are available for dogs. In the majority of cases, prescription drugs in carefully regulated doses can produce a remarkable improvement in the patient's condition. Euthanasia should not be considered for dogs with heart disease unless an adequate course of treatment with prescription drugs has failed to help the condition.

HEARTWORM INFECTION

Neither an owner nor a veterinarian can prevent the occurrence of most conditions affecting a dog's heart and lungs. Heartworm disease is the exception.

—

Heartworm infection can be prevented!
All dogs at risk should receive preventive medication.

—

Dirofilaria immitis is the parasite that infects both the dog and cat. Adult heartworms live in the chambers of the heart and in the major blood vessels of the patient. These parasites can be several inches in length and cause their damage by blocking the heart and vessels. The signs of advanced heartworm disease are the same as the signs of congestive heart failure: cough, tiring easily, sometimes edema (swelling) of the limbs.

Heartworms require months to mature in the dog's bloodstream, and dogs with early cases of heartworm infection often have no signs of illness. *Asymptomatic* cases of heartworm disease can be detected with a blood test and can be successfully cured with prescription drugs.

The heartworm life cycle is complicated and involves the mosquito as the intermediate host.

• Adult heartworms in the dog's bloodstream produce thousands of microscopic larvae called *microfilaria.*

• A mosquito that feeds upon an infected dog sucks up these microfilaria with the dog's blood.

• The microfilaria become infective in the salivary glands of the mosquito. When the mosquito feeds upon another dog, the infective microfilaria enter the bloodstream of that dog.

• These microfilaria eventually mature into adult heartworms in the heart and blood vessels of the second dog. These adult worms produce thousands of microfilaria. When a mosquito feeds on the second dog, the cycle is continued.

Heartworm preventive medication works by killing the microfilaria before they can become adults. Newer prescription medications are given once a month to destroy whatever microfilaria may be developing in the dog's bloodstream. Research has shown that if owners administer the medication with reasonable compliance with directions, almost 100 percent of dogs will be protected from this deadly parasite.

—

IMPORTANT NOTE:

Dogs over six months of age must have a negative blood test for the presence of heartworms before they are given the preventive drug. Serious side effects can occur if the drug is administered to a dog that is already infected with heartworm.

—

LUNG DISEASE

The primary signs of lung disease are the same as for most cardiovascular conditions; dyspnea, cough, and exercise intolerance. If a bacterial infection is present, fever will be present also.

Dogs are subject to almost the same diseases of the lung as are humans. Tumors of the lungs are not uncommon in older dogs. Although no evidence has been presented to indicate that dogs suffer ill effects from secondhand smoke, lung damage from environmental pollutants has been diagnosed. Viral and bacterial pneumonia can affect dogs. Coughs caused by allergies are not as common in dogs as in humans—allergic humans **cough,** allergic dogs **scratch.**

COUGH

Cough, in both dogs and humans, is a sign of a disease of the respiratory or cardiovascular system. Cough may be a more serious condition in dogs than in humans because there are no minor diseases that cause a dog to cough. Dogs do not catch cold or get the flu as do humans.

These are some of the more common causes of cough in the dog:

- Bacterial or viral pneumonia secondary to another disease such as canine distemper
- Pneumonia caused by foreign material in the lungs
- Upper respiratory conditions affecting the trachea and bronchi, such as the "kennel cough" complex of disease
- Congestive heart failure leading to an accumulation of fluid in the lungs
- Heartworms that mechanically obstruct circulation in the heart and major blood vessels
- Collapsed trachea, a condition that is not uncommon in elderly members of the toy breeds
- Primary or metastatic lung tumors

———

*A veterinarian should see every dog
with a chronic cough.*

———

Many of the conditions causing dogs to cough will escalate into life-threatening situations unless they are diagnosed accurately and treated appropriately.

Most coughing dogs cannot be helped by the administration of nonprescription *antitussives* (cough medicines). The cause of the cough must be treated before the cough can be expected to improve. Only a cough that originates in the trachea and bronchi of a dog may be lessened to some degree with an OTC human cough medicine. Pneumonia must be treated with antibiotics and supportive therapy, congestive heart failure with diuretics, and heartworm with antiparasitic drugs.

A cough may be *productive,* in which the patient brings up some fluid, or *nonproductive,* a dry, hacking cough in which no fluid is brought up. Coughing is often a sign of a seriously sick dog; all dogs that cough more than occasionally should be examined by a veterinarian.

"Kennel Cough"

The bacterium *Bordetella bronchiseptica* is the cause of a specific type of contagious disease in the dog, "kennel cough". This organism affects dogs' trachea and bronchi, typically producing a harsh, unproductive cough. Aerosol droplets spread the disease-causing bacteria from one dog to another. The disease is called kennel cough because it is common in boarding kennels and other places where dogs congregate. Diagnosis of this infection can usually be made from the history and signs: an owner phones his veterinarian to make an appointment for his dog, which "has something caught in its throat." The veterinarian immediately asks if the dog has been in a boarding kennel within the last ten days or has been exposed to other dogs. If so, then kennel cough is suspected.

A veterinarian will treat kennel cough with antibiotics to prevent secondary pneumonia and with antitussives to reduce the coughing. A vaccine exists for the prevention of some strains of *B. bronchiseptica;* however, since there are more than twenty separate strains of this organism, the vaccine may not be 100 percent effective in preventing the condition.

The use of human cough medicines is seldom effective in dogs. Only one nonprescription drug, *dextromethorphan hydrobromide,* is currently recognized as having value in treating cough in the dog. This drug is related to prescription-only opiate medications for dogs. It is important to note that the dog may require a completely different dose of opiates than does a human.

If a nonprescription cough suppressant must be given, the following common human medications may be given to dogs:

Cough Suppressants that May Be Useful in Treating "Kennel Cough"

DRUG	SOME BRAND NAMES	HOW SUPPLIED (LIQUIDS)
Dextromethorphan HBr	BENLYN ADULT	15 mg per tsp.
	BENLYN PEDIATRIC	7.5 mg per tsp.
	DELSYN	10 mg per tsp.
	PERTUSSIN	15 mg per tsp.
	ROBITUSSIN MAXIMUM STRENGTH	15 mg per tsp.
	ROBITUSSIN PEDIATRIC COUGH SUPPRESSANT	7.5 mg per tsp.

Dose: Approximately ½ to 1 mg per pound of body weight of the dog, with a maximum dose of 60 mg. Repeat every 12 hours if necessary. Discontinue the medication if the dog vomits or becomes very sleepy.

One standard measuring teaspoonful of liquid equals 5 cubic centimeters.

Many other brands and generics of this drug are available.

All these preparations are liquids. Liquids must be given slowly, to allow the dog to swallow the medication and to keep the medication from accidentally entering the dog's trachea. (See page 38 for instructions on administering liquid medication.)

15

THE URINARY AND REPRODUCTIVE SYSTEMS

—

No nonprescription medications are of value in treating conditions in this chapter.

—

No abnormalities or diseases of the canine urinary or reproductive systems are responsive to nonprescription, over-the counter medications. Disturbances of these systems can be life threatening and cannot be treated successfully except by qualified veterinary practitioners.

THE KIDNEYS

The filtering action of the kidneys removes waste products from the blood.

Fortunately, normal kidneys have a greater ability to remove toxins than the body actually needs. Almost every animal can live a normal life with just one healthy kidney. Only when the function of both kidneys is impaired does an animal becomes *uremic*. In uremia, toxic substances accumulate in the body. If the kidneys are damaged beyond function, *anuria* (not producing urine) results.

Bacterial disease, viral disease, or poisoning with *nephrotoxic* substances such as antifreeze are some of the causes of kidney failure. Early signs of kidney failure and uremia in the dog include anorexia and vomiting. Kidney stones, congenital abnormalities of the kidneys, and kidney tumors are problems that occur rarely in the dog. If any disease or condition of the kidneys is suspected, seek veterinary attention.

THE BLADDER

The dog suffering from infections and other bladder abnormalities will frequently exhibit signs that the owner can detect.

The bladder acts as a reservoir for urine produced by the kidneys. *Cystitis* indicates an inflammation of the bladder. Important signs of cystitis are frequent urination, straining while urinating, and blood in the urine *(hematuria.)* The presence and the cause of cystitis can be verified by a urinalysis performed by a veterinarian or a qualified technician. The presence or absence of blood cells, abnormal bladder cells, or crystals in the urine is used to make the diagnosis.

Bladder stones *(cystic calculi)* are common in dogs. Formed by the accumulation of certain minerals in the urine, bladder stones are more frequently found in females than in males, and are more common in certain breeds than in others. The dachshund and the miniature schnauzer appear to be overrepresented among cystic calculi patients.

Small bladder stones may be passed through the wider urethra of the female but may lodge and cause obstruction in the narrow male urethra. Larger stones remain in the bladder, where a single stone or multiple stones may fill the entire bladder cavity. Signs of bladder stones are similar to the signs of infectious cystitis: frequent urination, straining to urinate, and blood in the urine.

Diagnosis of cystic calculi is made by finding the stones on an X ray or finding the typical mineral crystals in the urine. A veterinarian can also often feel bladder stones through the patient's abdominal wall. Bladder stones in the dog are treated by one or both of two methods: surgical removal, or strict dietary alteration that causes the body to absorb the minerals of which the stones are composed. Your veterinarian will determine the best treatment based on the extent of the stones and the condition of the patient.

Incontinence is a condition in which the patient urinates involuntarily or dribbles urine. Incontinence is not the same as *submissive urination* displayed by excited puppies.

Incontinence caused by abnormal bladder conditions is not uncommon in older dogs. Because of a deficiency in hormones, older spayed dogs may urinate in their sleep. The presence or absence of this type of incontinence is not affected by the age at which the dog was spayed. Incontinence caused by hormone deficiency should be diagnosed by urinalysis to rule out cystitis, cystic calculi, or other problems. The condition is easily controlled by administration of small intermittent doses of prescription hormones.

THE FEMALE REPRODUCTIVE ORGANS

The primary female reproductive organs are the ovaries—the source of female hormones—fallopian tubes, and the uterus. Mammary glands are secondary female reproductive organs that are necessary to nourish the puppies after birth.

The female dog's normal *estrus* cycle occurs approximately twice a year. The dog's hormone cycle continues even if a fertile mating has not occurred. *Pseudocyesis,* or false pregnancy, occurs in the female dog at the termination of the normal gestation period of eight weeks. In many dogs, pseudocyesis has all the characteristics of a real pregnancy except for the birth of puppies, while in other dogs the signs of pseudocyesis are almost unnoticeable.

The cyclic nature of a female dog's hormone production has two extremely harmful effects upon the unspayed dog:

• The hormones might promote the development of *mammary tumors* (breast cancer). These tumors can be malignant. As tumors of the mammary glands are stimulated by the production of ovarian hormones, mammary tumors occur very commonly in older unspayed dogs. Primary ovarian tumors are rare in the canine species.

• In *septic metritis*, also termed *pyometra*, the uterus becomes filled with pus. This common life-threatening condition is caused by the action of ovarian hormones on the lining of the uterus of older unspayed female dogs. Without treatment, the dog can die of toxemia. A vaginal discharge is sometimes, but not always, present in cases of septic metritis.

Treatment for septic metritis is the surgical removal of the uterus and ovaries. Since the condition occurs in older, sick dogs, and these patients are poor surgical risks, extensive supportive therapy and prolonged hospitalization may be required if female dogs affected with septic metritis are to survive.

These conditions are compelling arguments to have a female dog spayed before her first heat period. Don't believe the old wives' tale that a female dog should be spayed only after it has had its first estrus. This belief is extremely detrimental to the future health of the dog. The spaying surgery is least risky to the dog when performed before it has reached sexual maturity. Mammary tumors, common in unspayed dogs, are almost unknown in dogs spayed before their first estrus period. Spaying a dog after it has undergone one or more heat periods will not prevent the formation of mammary tumors or the recurrence of those that have been surgically removed. Septic metritis cannot occur in a dog in which the uterus and ovaries have been surgically removed.

—

All female dogs that are not intended to reproduce should be spayed before their first heat.

—

THE MALE REPRODUCTIVE SYSTEM

The reproductive system of male dogs is subject to fewer problems than that of the female. *Cryptorchid* dogs are those with the testicles retained in the abdominal cavity or inguinal canal rather than descended into the normal position in the scrotum. *Monorchid* dogs are those with one descended, one retained testicle. While cryptorchid dogs are usually infertile, monorchid dogs are normally fertile. Both cryptorchidism and monorchidism are thought to be hereditary traits and are cause for disqualification in the show ring.

Sertoli cell tumors are not uncommon in dogs that have one or both retained testicles. The signs of Sertoli cell tumors may include the development of feminine characteristics as well as hair loss on the abdomen and trunk. Removal of the affected testes will cause these signs to disappear. Other testicular tumors are not common in the canine species.

Prostate cancer is uncommon in dogs, but benign *prostatic hyperplasia* occurs in many older, unneutered males. Signs of prostatic hyperplasia include difficulty in defecation, dribbling urine, and stilted, painful gait. Since male hormones influence prostatic hyperplasia, neutering of the dog is both preventive and curative.

Perianal adenomas are tumors that occur in the mucous membranes surrounding the anus of male dogs. These growths are almost unknown in female dogs. Perianal adenomas often become large, ulcerated, bleeding, and infected. Surgical removal of these growths is difficult because the area bleeds very readily and because sutures are disrupted by the patients when they lick the area or when they defecate.

As male hormones influence the development of perianal adenomas, these tumors occur very rarely in neutered dogs. Neutering, even without the removal of the tumors, will cause the growths to shrink in size, often to disappear entirely.

Urine scent-marking is a very common behavior in which male dogs mark their "territory" by urinating on objects in the house and yard. This undesirable action is sex related. Most dogs neutered before puberty will fully retain their guard-dog instincts but never develop the urine-marking behavior. Dogs neutered after marking behavior has become established often will retain the habit.

Although the physical problems associated with the male dog's reproductive system are fewer than the female's, to avoid the tendency to urine scent-mark in the house, veterinarians recommend that all pet dogs be neutered before they reach puberty at six or seven months of age. Allowing a pet dog to remain unneutered until it can develop masculine characteristics allows it to develop only one thing: *bad habits.*

—

**NO NONPRESCRIPTION MEDICATIONS
ARE OF USE FOR CONDITIONS
DESCRIBED IN THIS CHAPTER**

—

APPENDIX I

THE USE OF HERBS IN CANINE MEDICINE

Man's very first medicines were medicinal herbs. Since before recorded time, people have eaten, drunk, and applied to their bodies plant materials that they hoped had powers to alleviate disease and to heal injury. How did this practice come about? Perhaps humans may have observed that animals included certain plants in their diets without harmful results. These early herbalists then set out to discover the therapeutic value of the same plants. Eventually a body of medical lore developed, passed down through generations and fostered by tradition and the tribal elders. We do know that the use of herbs in religious ceremonies dates back thousands of years.

HERBS ARE THE SOURCE OF SOME MODERN MEDICINES

Today, some of our best-known and most widely used medications were originally herbal products. Pharmacists call these drugs *botanicals,* meaning that they are made from plants. Many modern botanicals are synthesized in the laboratory; often these synthetic botanicals are superior in purity, efficacy, and standardized strength.

- *Aspirin* is made from willow bark. It has been on the market since 1899.
- *Atropine,* a drug that affects some parts of the nervous system, is made from the belladonna plant, also known as "deadly nightshade."

- *Caffeine* is extracted from coffee beans.
- *Codeine* and *morphine* are painkillers that are made from the opium poppy.
- *Quinine,* a drug used to treat malaria, is made from the bark of a tree.
- *Digitoxin,* a common heart medication, is made from foxglove.
- *Penicillin,* the first antibiotic ever discovered, comes from a common mold.

THE PLACEBO EFFECT

The dictionary defines a placebo as "a preparation containing no medicine but given for its psychological effect." In other words, a placebo is a nonmedicinal preparation that a patient is led to believe will make him better. Improvement in the condition of the patient receiving only the placebo may be the result of the power of suggestion. Human patients think that they will get better, so they actually feel that they get better.

Obviously, dogs are not *placebo-responders*. Explaining to a dog that a medicine will improve its condition is not likely to influence the results. However, while dogs do not respond to the power of suggestion, owners certainly do. It has been shown that more than 30 percent of humans receiving placebos feel that they are helped by the preparation. Since people tend to identify closely with their dogs, it is likely that if dogs were to be given placebos, more than 30 percent of their owners would feel that their dogs' conditions were improved.

SPONTANEOUS OR NATURAL HEALING

The sale of herbs is a billion-dollar business in the United States. People buy and use herbs because they are led to believe that the preparations will prevent or cure medical conditions, or will increase their energy level, their sexual performance, or their general well-being. Is this money well spent? In many cases it is hard to tell.

Herbs are seldom taken for medical conditions that are of immediate threat to life. People elect to use herbal therapy because they would like to have more energy, sleep better, eliminate intestinal gas, or obtain relief from other relatively trivial complaints. Physicians recognize that medical problems of this type tend to disappear even without treatment. Herbologists credit apparent cures to the action of herbs when the cures may be the result of the body's ability to heal itself even without drugs or the placebo effect.

Most herbal preparations have not yet been tested in such a way that the placebo effect is eliminated. These herbs rely on anecdotal "evidence" to demonstrate their value. Many of these anecdotes, however, number in the thousands and encompass many years, even centuries, of human experience. Medical science recognizes that all old wives' tales are not empty of value. Recent controlled studies of a few of the more commonly used herbs suggest that some may actually be beneficial. Selected herbal products may eventually enter the list of drugs that are proven useful against the ailments of both humans and animals.

HERBAL PREPARATIONS ARE NOT REGULATED BY THE FDA

The federal Food and Drug Administration does not consider herbal preparations to be drugs. The FDA classifies herbs as dietary supplements or foodstuffs. Therefore the production, licensing, and sale of herbs are not subject to the regulations of the FDA.

As makers of dietary supplements, producers of herbal substances are not required to demonstrate that their products are effective in the treatment of any medical condition, nor are herbal products required to meet government standards of ingredients or of purity. Herbal preparations are not even required to demonstrate lack of toxicity. Buyers of herbal preparations have no governmental assurance that these products actually contain the substances listed in the strengths indicated on the labels.

Major suppliers of herbs may qualify statements that claim effectiveness of their products with phrases such as this:

—

"THIS STATEMENT HAS NOT BEEN EVALUATED BY THE FOOD AND DRUG ADMINISTRATION."

—

CHARACTERISTICS OF HERBAL CLAIMS

• The reader of herbal literature will notice that it is never claimed that the products have any direct medical benefits. Terminology such as "may help," "may aid," "assists in healing," and similar nondefinitive statements is often used.

A major chain of natural health "supplements" labels its merchandise in "servings" rather than in doses to emphasize that the products they sell are not considered drugs. The colorful catalog of another prominent herb supply company includes this disclaimer on every page:

—

"THIS PRODUCT IS NOT INTENDED TO DIAGNOSE, TREAT, CURE, OR PREVENT ANY DISEASE"

—

• Herbal claims are often expressed in undefined terms. What is the scientific meaning of "cleansing"? What is the meaning of "soothing," "calming," or "strengthening"? Of "quickens" or "purifies"?

• A single herb may be claimed to have therapeutic value for many very different conditions. For example, echinacea is one of the best-selling herbs on the market today. This herb is claimed to be beneficial for such diverse conditions as tonsillitis, blood poisoning, microbial infection, asthma, and snakebite. Another herb, kavakava, is used to treat nervousness, anxiety, insomnia, gonorrhea, rheumatism, and gout! Some herbs are even claimed to be beneficial both when taken internally and when applied to the skin.

• Many herbal preparations have the same claims of action. For example, elderberry, hawthorn, kelp, and senna (as well as psyllium, which is proven to be effective) are all claimed to be remedies for constipation.

• Herbologists (people who use, recommend, and sell herbs) often disparage conventional medicine. One well-known author decries the use of vaccines. Another recommends a seven-day fast as a cure for canine distemper. Herbologists often promote "natural" diets for dogs, including the feeding of only raw meat.

• Commercial herbal preparations often contain many ingredients. The "shotgun" effect is offered to convince consumers that at least one component will produce the desired results.

HERBS FOR DOGS

Pyrethrins and rotenone, both herbal products, were among the first safe and effective insecticides available to control fleas and other external parasites on animals. These preparations are still in wide use, although modern synthetic insecticides are available that have far greater efficacy and duration of action. When used correctly, the more effective drugs pose no greater danger to the host or to the environment (but far greater danger to the parasite) than do the herbal products.

Various citrus derivatives are sold in shampoos as flea repellants. Their value is limited at best. Herbal scents in dog shampoos are more appealing to owners than they are discouraging to fleas.

Herbal flea collars, even those that can be "recharged" with solutions of herbs, have not been found to be of major benefit in repelling or controlling fleas on dogs.

"Behavior altering" herbs such as Saint-John's-wort have been administered to dogs as a tranquilizing agent. The effect of this treatment is probably dependent upon the placebo-responsiveness of the owners.

THE USE OF HERBS CAN BE HARMFUL TO DOGS

• Certain herbs can cause toxic reactions. For example, if given in excessive quantities or for a prolonged period of time, ephedra may cause nervousness and possibly convulsions in both dogs and humans. Moreover, the correct dose of ephedra for dogs has never been determined.

• Patients seeking herbal "cures" may postpone conventional medical treatment until their conditions are so far advanced that a successful outcome may be difficult or impossible. Owners treating their dogs with herbs may delay appropriate veterinary treatment until it is too late to help their pets.

• Many herbs, particularly those reputed to be "soothing" or "calming," may interact dangerously with prescription or nonprescription drugs. Herbs should never be taken with or given with other drugs without the advice of a physician or a veterinarian. Herbs should not be taken with alcoholic beverages, a factor that seldom needs to be considered when medicating dogs.

• It is never safe to apply any data obtained from humans to the use of a substance in another species. A dog is not a small, furry human. Substances and doses that humans tolerate very well may be deadly to dogs.

• The consumer's wallet may suffer major damage. Herbs are not inexpensive. Money spent at a health-food store may be more appropriately applied to conventional nutritional and medical products.

HERBAL PREPARATIONS

The majority of commercial herb preparations on the market are in the form of dried, powdered herbs. These are usually sold in capsule form; some are sold in small bulk packages. It is likely that heat-drying or even freeze-drying destroys a great deal of the activity of the preparations.

Herbal infusions, teas, tinctures, and brews are extractions of herbs in water, alcohol, or various oils. Most preparations designed to be taken internally are water based. Salves and cremes intended to be applied to the skin are often oil or petrolatum based.

Fresh herbs in bunches or in cellophane packages are available during the late summer in some markets. Dedicated herbologists cultivate herbs in their home gardens or in pots on their windowsills.

Herbal shampoos are nothing more than detergent-based shampoos to which are added herbal extracts as scents or insecticides. Except in the case of pyrethrins or rotenone, it is unlikely that the addition of herbs is effective in controlling parasites.

Herbs in Common Usage for Humans and Dogs

HERB	EFFECT CLAIMED
Alfalfa	blood purifier, arthritis
Aloe vera	skin lesions
Anise	expectorant, reduce coughing
Bilberry	diarrhea, blood disorders

Herbs in Common Usage for Humans and Dogs (*continued*)

HERB	EFFECT CLAIMED
Catnip	fever, colic, insomnia, stress, general tonic
Coltsfoot	skin disorders
Chamomile	nerve "tonic"
Cranberry	urinary-tract health
Dandelion	general tonic and diuretic
Echinacea	disorders of lymphatic system
Ephedra	circulatory & cardiovascular stimulant
Evening primrose	obesity
Feverfew	migrane headaches
Ginger	motion sickness
Garlic	antibiotic, detoxifies the body
Ginkgo biloba	mental alertness
Ginseng	impotence, increases energy
Goldenseal	canker sores, indigestion
Kavakava	nervousness, insomnia
Kelp	constipation, stress, blood purifier
Licorice	gastric ulcers
Milk thistle	liver disorders
Parsley	obesity, rheumatism, edema, indigestion
Peppermint	nausea, gastritis, and even tumors(!)
Pyrethrins	insecticide
Rotenone	insecticide
Saw palmetto	antiseptic
Saint-John's-wort	depression, anxiety, anti-inflammatory

APPENDIX II

ACCIDENTAL POISONING

—

Ingestion, inhalation, and skin contact can result in poisoning see page 247 for poison control centers.

—

FOOD POISONING

If humans eat it, will it harm dogs? The answer can be *yes*. Few items of humans' diets are actually harmful to dogs, but dogs will eat human food products in forms that no human would touch. Dogs are not discriminating in the selection or amount of the substances they will eat if they find the odor attractive.

• **Leftover Food:** Owners often feed food scraps, grease, and bones to their pet with the mistaken idea that they are giving the dog a "treat." The familiar "Thanksgiving and Christmas vomiting and diarrhea syndrome" caused by the family dog eating holiday leftovers is the prime example of a condition caused by this overindulgence.

Toxic agent: Bones, grease, and skin contain no toxic agents unless the food material has started to spoil. The malfunction of the affected dog's digestive tract is caused by an overload of fats and indigestible substances.

Signs: Vomiting and diarrhea, the severity of which depends
upon two factors: the amount of leftovers consumed in relation to the size of the dog, and the sensitivity of the individual animal.

Treatment: Withholding food for twelve to twenty-four hours
usually will return the patient to normal. Danger signs that indicate veterinary care is needed include vomiting and diarrhea
that persist after the patient's stomach has emptied of the irritating material. A veterinarian should see any dog that has persistent unproductive vomiting, or diarrhea that contains blood.

• **Garbage:** Bacteria thrive and produce toxins in spoiled
food. Decaying food therefore contains toxins that can be
more harmful to dogs than greasy leftovers. Some dogs poisoned by spoiled meat will not survive without emergency
medical care.

Toxic agents: Bacterial toxins produced by Salmonella and certain other bacteria contained by the garbage.

Signs: Severe and persistent vomiting and diarrhea. Vomiting
blood or blood in stool. Dehydration with tucked-up abdomen.
Reluctance to move, and other signs of abdominal pain.

Treatment: Dogs suffering from bacterial toxemia require supportive therapy such as intravenous fluids and antibiotics.
Veterinary treatment is required.

• **Botulism:** eating improperly preserved home-canned
food often causes Botulism in humans. Eating the spoiled
carcasses of animals killed on the road most frequently
causes botulism in dogs.

Toxic agent: Nerve toxins produced within the cells of the organism *Clostridium botulinum*.

Signs: Dogs that consume these bacteria may initially vomit the material consumed. The animal will show signs of progressive weakness and incoordination if much of the toxin is absorbed into the blood. Eventually the animal may be unable to stand. Death can occur from respiratory paralysis

Treatment: Botulism is an emergency. The affected dog should be rushed to the nearest veterinary facility.

• **Meat wrappings and greasy steel wool:** If it smells like meat or grease, dogs are likely to eat it. Chewed-up butcher's paper may or may not pass through a dog's intestines. The dog that eats steel wool cannot escape serious mechanical damage to its intestinal tract.

Toxic agent: Mechanical damage to the intestinal tract.

Signs: Severe abdominal pain, vomiting blood, rectal bleeding.

Treatment: Veterinary treatment, which may include surgery, is required.

• **Tea and coffee:** Both contain chemical stimulants that are bad for dogs. Tea bags and coffee grounds in garbage are a potential source of toxicity to a dog.

Toxic agent: Caffeine, theophylline, and theobromine.

Signs: The severity of the signs depends on the amount of the material consumed. Excitement, nervousness, muscle spasm, seizures, and hyperthermia (increased body temperature) are possible.

Treatment: Veterinary treatment is recommended for severely affected dogs.

• **Chocolate:** The chemicals contained in chocolate are toxic to dogs. Baking chocolate contains more of these substances than does milk chocolate. The toxic dose for a small dog can be as little as two or three squares of baking chocolate.

Toxic agent: Theobromine and caffeine.

Signs: Similar to those of tea and coffee.

Treatment: Veterinary treatment is recommended for severely affected dogs.

POISONOUS PLANTS

• **House plants** such as amaryllis, asparagus fern, crown of thorns, some ivy plants, chrysanthemum plants.

Toxic agents: Many different poisons.

Signs: Vomiting, abdominal pain, tremors, convulsions, and increased respiratory rate.

Treatment: Only veterinary treatment may be effective.

• **Outdoor plants** such as castor beans, daffodil, bittersweet, Indian tobacco, azalea, cherry laurel, hemlock, oleander, yew, and many others.

Toxic agent: The poisonous substance depends on the species of plant consumed.

Signs: Vomiting and diarrhea.

Treatment: Call poison center and seek veterinary attention.

• **Poisonous mushrooms** are often used as playthings by puppies and young dogs. If the dog consumes much of a poisonous mushroom, signs may be apparent in ten to fourteen hours. Large, showy mushrooms of the *Amanita* genus are often implicated. Suspect mushroom poisoning in dogs that play in damp woodlands in the summer and fall.

Toxic agents: Various substances affect internal organs such as the kidney and liver, or affect the nervous system.

Signs: Common signs of mushroom poisoning are abdominal pain, vomiting, and diarrhea that last a day or two before the development of liver and kidney failure that may cause convulsions, coma, and death.

Treatment: If a dog is suspected of eating mushrooms, vomiting should be induced (see page 152). The local poison control center and a veterinarian should be consulted.

CHEMICAL POISONS

• **Cleaning products:** Curious dogs occasionally lick dishwasher granules, oven cleaners, toilet bowl cleaners, furniture polishes, shoe polishes, and floor polishes. Bleach, ammonia, detergents, drain openers (lye), kerosene, paint stripper and removers, paint thinners, gasoline, and wood preservatives are other substances with which a dog may come in contact or consume.

Toxic agents: Caustics that destroy tissues by acid or alkaline burns. Depending on the substance involved, toxic agents may be absorbed into the animals' bloodstream and damage many structures of the body.

Signs: Burns in the mouth and throat or on the skin accompanied by damage to the stomach, intestines, and other internal organs. This damage causes bloody vomiting and diarrhea.

Treatment: Flush the skin and mouth with plain water to wash away the chemicals. *Do not induce vomiting.* Call the local poison control center.

• **Ethylene glycol antifreeze** has a sweet taste. When it is leaked from a car radiator or spilled on the ground, dogs often consume it. Ethylene glycol is extremely toxic. The dog that consumes only a half teaspoonful of ethylene glycol per pound of its body weight will have severe damage to its nervous system and kidneys.

Toxic agent: Ethylene glycol.

Signs: Dogs affected with antifreeze poisoning show ataxia (loss of coordination), vomiting, collapse, convulsions, and coma. These signs occur soon after ingestion. If treatment is not initiated immediately, irreversible damage to the dog's kidneys occurs within thirty-six hours.

Treatment: Veterinary treatment must be started as soon as possible.

• **Chlorine tablets or powder** that are used to purify swimming pools may be eaten or licked off paws by dogs.

Signs: Vomiting, diarrhea, and inflammation of the mouth, tongue, and eyes.

Treatment: The eyes and mouth should be rinsed with copious quantities of water. A veterinarian should be consulted immediately.

• **Lead poisoning** occurs in dogs that chew fishing weights, curtain weights, old lead paint on wood or metal, and lead pipes or pipes that have lead solder on them.

Signs: Vomiting may or may not occur. Diarrhea and evidence of abdominal pain may be seen later. The signs may progress to nervousness, hysteria, fear of light, incoordination, and partial paralysis.

Treatment: If ingestion of lead is suspected, vomiting should be induced with baking soda or hydrogen peroxide. A veterinarian can determine by use of a blood test if lead poisoning is occurring. Antidotes administered by a veterinarian can be lifesaving.

PESTICIDES

• **Rat and mouse poisoned bait or animals that have died from eating poisoned bait** are occasionally eaten by dogs.

Toxic agents: Warfain, sodium fluoroacetate, strychnine, ANTU, Bromethalin, cholecalciferol, phosphorus, red squill, zinc phosphide, and aluminum phosphide.

Signs: The signs depend upon the agent consumed. Anticoagulant rodent poisons cause death by internal and external bleeding. The dog may show nasal bleeding, bleeding from the rectum, vomiting blood, and blood in the urine. Other signs are weakness, incoordination, evidence of abdominal pain, and rapid breathing.
  Poisons that do not contain anticoagulants usually affect the nervous system. Hyperexcitability, muscle tremors, and seizures can occur. Some other agents affect the kidneys and heart.
  Phosphorus-containing poisons damage the liver. Early

signs of phosphorus poisoning are vomiting with severe and often bloody diarrhea. Signs of liver damage are severe abdominal pain and a yellow color to the skin and mouth. Phosphorus poisoning is usually fatal.

Treatment: Rush to a veterinarian. Animals often die from eating rat and mouse poisons.

• **Ant poisons** are commonly used around houses and yards. Dogs may lick the poisons directly or lick poison-covered paws.

Toxic agents: Organophosphates or carbamates.

Signs: Muscle tremors, nervousness, and convulsions.

Treatment: Only veterinary treatment may be successful.

• **Snail baits in powders, granules, or pellets** may be eaten by dogs. Dogs apparently enjoy the taste of snail bait and eat it willingly.

Toxic agent: Metaldehyde

Signs: Excess salivation, tremors, rapid breathing, convulsions, coma, and death.

Treatment: Emergency veterinary treatment is required.

• **Flea and tick preparations** can be harmful if misused. Every product must be used strictly according to the manufacturer's directions. Using too much of a product, using a product too often, or using it on animals that are too young for the product may cause extremely severe reactions. In some cases, misuse of insecticides can cause animals' death.

POISONING BY NONSTEROIDAL ANTI-INFLAMMATORY DRUGS

• **Aspirin, acetaminophen, ibuprophin, or naproxen.**
Poisoning with these drugs may occur when a dog is given
an excessive dose of an NSAID for pain control.

Signs: The affected animal refuses food, is depressed, and has
abdominal pain. The dog may also have vomiting with or
without blood, and be uncoordinated.

Treatment: Since the agent is known, induce vomiting by giving baking soda or hydrogen peroxide within an hour. The
patient should have veterinary attention as soon as possible.

HUMAN MOOD-ALTERING DRUGS

• **Sedatives, antianxiety drugs, and antidepressants** may
be given to dogs by people who think the drugs will calm the
dog. Dogs may also accidentally eat their owners' medication.

Signs: Some mood-altering human drugs cause depression
and incoordination in dogs. Other drugs cause excitement,
restlessness, and agitation. The ingestion of human mood-
altering drugs may result in dogs becoming comatose. Large
doses of these drugs may be fatal.

Treatment: If it is known that the dog ingested a mood-altering
drug, vomiting should be induced. Feeding activated charcoal may also be helpful to absorb some of the drug. Affected animals should be kept warm. A severely depressed
animal should be rushed to an emergency clinic.

• **Illicit mood-altering drugs** such as marijuana *(cannabis),*
amphetamines, cocaine, and other psychedelic drugs may be

administered to dogs by human drug abusers. Dogs also may accidentally find and consume these drugs.

Signs: Incoordination, fear biting, dilated pupils, salivation, agitation, and depression.

Treatment: Immediate veterinary attention!

INHALED POISONS

• **Carbon monoxide** from improperly vented furnaces and heating devices.

Toxic agent: Carbon monoxide.

Signs: Incoordination, rapidly followed by unconsciousness.

Treatment: Remove the dog from the source of fumes. Seek veterinary attention if the animal does not regain consciousness within a few minutes.

• **Toxic fumes produced by burning plastics** can cause asphyxiation or poisoning by inhaled chemicals.

Toxic agents: Specific for the material that is burned.

Signs: Depression, incoordination, panting, coughing, deep red color to gums, difficult breathing, and convulsions.

Treatment: Keep the dog's airway open, give cardiopulmonary resuscitation, keep patient warm, and get immediate veterinary help.

SKIN CONTACT POISONS

• **Petroleum products** such as gasoline, paint, paint thinner, motor oil, and organic solvents can cause irritation and damage to the skin. If the dog licks the substance, it will cause irritation to the inside of the mouth. If swallowed, petroleum products may cause internal poisoning.

Signs: Skin irritation, licking of fur, salivation, and incoordination. Paint, but not solvents, may be seen on the hair or skin. Solvents may emit a characteristic odor.

Treatment: DO NOT remove paint from dogs' skin or coat with solvents. Instead, rub large amounts of mineral oil or vegetable oil into the contaminated area to soften and absorb the toxic material. When the material is softened, wash the dog with mild shampoo and warm water. Clipping or shaving should be used to remove paint that is only on the coat.

• **Salt or chemicals that melt ice** on roads and paths may be licked off contaminated paws.

Toxic agents: Usually sodium chloride or potassium chloride.

Signs: Vomiting.

Treatment: Wash chemicals off paws. Withhold food until vomiting has stopped.

GLOSSARY OF TERMS
AS USED IN THIS BOOK

acute: having a rapid onset.

allergen: a substance that causes an allergic response.

ambulate, ambulation: to walk or run.

analgesia: without pain.

analgesic: a drug that relieves pain.

anconeal process: a portion of the bone of the elbow.

anesthesia: a state of temporary unconsciousness or insensitivity.

anesthetic: a substance that renders an animal temporarily unconscious.

ankylosis: joined together, usually an abnormal fusion of bones.

anorexia: lack of desire or reluctance to eat.

antiemetics: medications to stop vomiting.

antigen: a protein substance that causes the body to produce immune antibodies.

antimicrobial agent: a substance that acts against microbes.

antiseborrheic: a subject that acts to remove oily substances on the skin.

antitussive: a drug that reduces coughing.

anuria: not producing urine.

arthritis: inflammation of a joint, often accompanied by pain, swelling, and calcium deposits on the joint surfaces.

articular surfaces: bony surfaces that come together to form joints.

asymptomatic: without symptoms or signs.

ataxia: incoordination or staggering.

ataxic: the state of being uncoordinated.

attenuated: weakened or killed, usually refers to bacteria or viruses in vaccines.

auricle: the portion of the ear outside of the skull; also called the pinna.

benign: not harmful, recurrent, or progressive; usually refers to tumors.

biopsy (n): a portion of tissue removed for microscopic examination.

biopsy (v): to remove a small piece of tissue for microscopic examination.

brand-name drug: a drug sold under patent.

bronchi, bronchial tubes: passages from the trachea to the lungs.

caloric density: the amount of calories present in a given amount of food.

CAT scan: computerized axial tomography study.

cecum: a portion of the intestinal tract analogous to the appendix in humans.

cerumen: waxy material produced by the epithelial cells of the external ear canal in response to irritation.

cervical: pertaining to the neck.

chronic: present for a long period of time.

coccygeal: pertaining to the tail.

complete fracture: a bone that is broken into two or more separate pieces.

congenital: a trait that is present at birth but that may not become apparent until later in life.

conjunctiva: the tissue surrounding the eyeball and lining the lids of the eye.

contagious: transmissible from one animal to another.

contraindicated: not recommended.

cornea: the outer transparent layer of the eyeball.

cortex: the outer layer of a bone.

crepitation: the crackling or grating sound heard or felt when broken bones or arthritic joints are moved.

cubic centimeter, milliliter: a unit of fluid measure equal to

1/1,000 of a liter; a measuring teaspoon contains approximately 5 cubic centimeters or 5 milliliters.

cystitis: an inflammation of the urinary bladder.

debride: to remove debris, to decontaminate.

defecate: to move the bowels.

dermatitis: inflammation of the skin; a skin disease.

dermis: the layers of the skin beneath the epidermis.

digits: fingers and toes.

dysplasia: abnormal formation of a part of the body (Greek *dys,* "bad"; *plasia,* "formation").

dysplastic: the state of having dysplasia.

dyspnea: difficult breathing.

dystocia: difficult birth.

ectoparasite: a parasite that lives in or on the skin of the host.

eczema: inflammatory superficial dermatitis that may be acute or chronic.

emesis: vomiting.

epidermis: the outer nonvascular layer of the skin.

estrus, estrus cycle: reproductive or "heat" cycle.

excised: cut away; surgically removed.

excrement: feces, stool, bowel movements.

extra-label use: used for purposes not specified on the label.

feces, fecal material: stool, bowel movements.

femur: thigh bone.

fetid: smell of putrefaction.

forceps: surgical instruments resembling scissors but designed to grasp instead of to cut.

gastritis: inflammation of the lining of the stomach.

generic drug: a drug that is not under patent.

gram: a unit of weight equal to 1/1,000 of a kilogram.

greenstick fracture: a fracture broken through only one cortex of a bone.

herbologist: a person who studies or advocates the use of herbs.

hematuria: blood in the urine.

hemorrhage: bleeding.

host: an animal upon which a parasite lives.

host-specific parasite: a parasite that lives only on one species of animal.

hyperkeratosis: excess growth of the outer layer of the skin.

hyperthermia: increased body temperature.

idiopathic: of unknown cause.

infectious: capable of being spread to other animals.

ingested: eaten, licked.

inherited: passed from the parents to the offspring.

instill: to put in.

integument: the skin.

intermediate host: an animal in or on which a parasite passes all or part of its larval stages.

intervertebral disc: the fibrous material between the vertebrae.

intralesional: inside a sore or lesion.

intrauterine: occurring in the uterus before birth.

kennel cough: a disease caused by the organism *Bordetella bronchiseptica*.

kilogram: a unit of weight equal to 2.2 pounds.

laceration: a cut or wound.

lame: of impaired ability to walk or run.

lateral: toward the outside of the body.

lesion: a wound, injury, or sore; an abnormal area.

liter: a unit of fluid measure equal to a little more than a quart.

lumbar: pertaining to the lower back.

luxated (v), luxation (n): displaced or dislocated; not in the correct position; usually refers to joints.

macroscopic: visible without magnification.

malignant: has potential to invade tissue.

malocclusion: improper placement of the teeth.

margin of safety: the amount of a substance that can be used before it becomes toxic.

medial: toward the midline of the body.

megaesophagus: an abnormally dilated esophagus.

metacarpal bones: bones of the wrist.

metatarsal bones: bones of the ankle.

metritis: an inflammation of the uterus.

microbe: a microscopic organism.

milligram: a unit of weight equal to 1/100 of a gram.

milliliter: a unit of liquid measure equal to approximately 1/30 of an ounce.

motile: capable of motion.

MRI: magnetic resonance imaging.

nasal: pertaining to the nose.

negatively geotropic: a tendency to move upward away from the ground.

nephrotoxic: damaging to the kidneys.

nonviable: unable to live.

NPD: the abbreviation for nonprescription drug.

NSAID: the abbreviation for nonsteroidal anti-inflammatory drug.

oblique fracture: a bone that is broken on an angle.

obstipation: the complete blockage of the lower bowel with foreign material such as bone fragments.

occular: pertaining to the eye.

OFA: the abbreviation for Orthopedic Foundation for Animals.

olecranon: the bony point of the elbow.

ophthalmic: pertaining to the eye; a medication designed for use in the eye.

oral medication: taken or administered by mouth.

osteosarcoma: cancer of the bone.

OTC: abbreviation for over the counter.

OTC drugs: drugs sold without prescription.

otic: pertaining to the ear.

otitis: infection of the ear.

ovum (plural: ova): egg.

palliative: a substance that relieves the signs without curing the condition.

palpation: feeling, examining by feel.

paralysis: complete loss of motor function of a part or all of the body.

parasite: an organism that lives in or on another organism.

parasiticides: drugs that kill parasites.

paresis: partial paralysis.

patella: the kneecap.

pathogenic: capable of causing disease.

pelvis: the hip bones.

photophobia: sensitivity to light; the avoidance of light.

placebo: a preparation identical in appearance to a medication but containing no active ingredients.

placebo effect: the improvement in a patient's condition due entirely to the power of suggestion.

positively geotropic: having the tendency to travel toward the ground.

proglottid: a segment of a tapeworm.

prolapse: a structure that protrudes into another space.

protozoa: a one-celled organism.

pruritus: itching.

pseudocyesis: a condition in which an animal has the signs of pregnancy but is not actually pregnant; also called "false" pregnancy.

purulent: containing pus.

pyoderma: pus in the skin; a skin infection accompanied by pus.

radiograph: a X ray.

radius and ulna: the bones of the lower arm or front limb.

residual: remaining for a period of time.

scapula: the shoulder blade.

sebum: the material produced by the sebaceous glands of the skin.

sedative: a substance that renders an animal relatively unresponsive.

shock: a condition of acute circulatory failure.

signs: indications of disease or abnormality in animals that can be detected by owners and veterinarians.

spondylitis: an inflammation of a joint.

spondylosis: abnormal bone growth that joins two bones that are normally separate.

stifle: the knee joint.

swimmer: a puppy of three weeks or older that cannot support its weight on its hind legs.

symptoms: subjective signs that can be expressed verbally by human patients.

testis (plural: testes): the testicles.

therapeutic: a substance or action that helps to cure or alleviate an abnormal condition.

thoracic: pertaining to the chest.

thorax: the chest.

tibia and fibula: the bones of the lower leg or hind limb.

topical medication: a substance applied to the skin.

toxic: poisonous.

trachea: the windpipe.

transverse fracture: a fracture in which a bone is broken straight through both sides.

trauma: violent injury.

ulcerated cornea: damaged area that appears white, often with a depression in the center.

ununited: not joined.

uremia: a condition caused by toxic substances in the blood as the result of impaired kidney function.

urinary incontinence: involuntary urination.

urticaria: a blood-vessel reaction in the skin that results in raised areas and is frequently accompanied by severe itching; hives.

vector: a carrier.

vehicle: a substance in which the active ingredients of a drug are suspended.

vermifuge: a medication that kills or expels intestinal parasites.

vertebra (plural: vertebrae): bones of the spine.

vomitus: material that is vomited.

whelp (n): a puppy, especially a newborn puppy.

whelp (v): to give birth. A term used for the canine species.

X ray: a radiographic picture of bones or internal structures of the body.

zoonosis: diseases communicable from animals to humans under natural conditions.

BIBLIOGRAPHY

Carlson, Delbert G., D.V.M. and James M. Giffin, M.D. *Dog Owner's Home Veterinary Handbook*. New York: Howell Book House, 1992.

Chandler, Asa C., M.S. Ph.D. *Introduction to Parasitology*. New York: John Wiley & Sons, 1995.

Dorland, W. A. Newman. *Dorland's Illustrated Medical Dictionary*. Philadelphia and London: W. B. Saunders Company, 1995.

Foster, Race, D.V.M., and Marty Smith, D.V.M. *Just What the Doctor Ordered: A Complete Guide to Drugs and Medications for Your Dog*. New York: Howell Book House, 1996.

Fudyma, Janice. *What Do I Take? A Consumer's Guide to Nonprescription Drugs*. New York: HarperPerennial, 1997.

Griffith, H. Winter, M.D. *Complete Guide to Prescription and Nonprescription Drugs*. New York: The Body Press/Perigree Books, 1998.

Koutz, F. R., and R. E. Rebrassier. *Identification and Life Cycles of Parasites Affecting Domestic Animals*. Columbus, OH: Ohio State University Press, 1948.

Levy, Juliette de Bairacli. *The Complete Herbal Handbook for the Dog and Cat,* sixth edition. London and Boston: Faber and Faber, 1991. First published in 1955.

Lincoff, Gary H. *The Audubon Society Field Guide to North American Mushrooms*. New York: Alfred A. Knopf, 1981.

MacCarthy, Alan W., Jr. *How to Save Big Buck$ on Your Pet's Veterinary Bills*. Palo Alto, CA: First Care! Company Publications, 1996.

The Merck Veterinary Manual, eighth edition. Whitehouse Station, NJ: Merck and Co., 1998.

Muller, George H., D.V.M., and Robert W. Kirk, D.V.M. *Small Animal Dermatology.* Philadelphia: W. B. Sanders Company, 1969.

Niering, William A., and Nancy C. Olmstead. *The Audubon Society Field Guide to North American Wildflowers.* New York: Alfred A Knopf, 1979.

Physician's Desk Reference for Nonprescription Drugs, 19th edition. Montvale, NJ: Medical Economics Company, 1998.

Physician's Desk Reference, 53rd edition. Montvale, NJ: Medical Economics Company, 1999.

Pitcarin, Richard H., D.V.M., Ph.D. and Susan Pitcarin Hubble. *Dr. Pitcarin's Complete Guide to Natural Health for Dogs and Cats.* Emmaus, PA: Rodale Press, revised 1995.

Plumb, Donald C., *Veterinary Drug Handbook,* third edition. White Bear Lake, MN: Pharm Vet Publishing, 1999.

Reinhart, Gregory A., Ph.D., and Daniel P. Carey. *Recent Advances in Canine and Feline Nutrition, Volume II. 1998 Iams Nutrition Symposium Proceedings.* Wilmington, OH: Orange Frazier Press, 1998.

Rosenfeld, Isadore, M.D. *Dr. Rosenfeld's Guide to Alternative Medicine.* New York: Random House, 1995.

Schoen, Allen M., and Susan G. Wynn. *Complementary and Alternative Veterinary Medicine: Principles and Practice.* St. Louis, MO: Mosby-Year Book, 1997.

Sisson, Septimus, and James Daniel Grossman. *The Anatomy of the Domestic Animals,* fourth edition. Philadelphia and London: W. B. Saunders Company, 1953.

Steadman, Thomas Lathrop. *Steadman's Medical Dictionary,* 26th edition. Baltimore, MD: Williams and Wilkens, 1990.

Thomas, Robert H. *Tabers Cyclopedic Medical Dictionary,* 18th edition. Philadelphia: F. A. Davis Company, 1998.

Veterinary Pharmaceuticals and Biologicals, 11th edition. Montvale, NJ: Medical Economics Company, 1999–2000.

ORGANIZATIONS CONCERNED WITH CANINE HEALTH ISSUES

HELP IN CASES OF SUSPECTED POISONING

—

National Animal Poison Control Center
24-Hour Hot lines:
(900) 680-0000
(800) 548-2423
(888) 426-4425

—

A veterinary toxicologist is always on duty. There is a charge per case, which can be applied to a credit card or a telephone bill.

—

Local Poison Control Center 24-Hour Hot line:
Find the telephone number in the white pages of the local telephone book under "Emergency Numbers"

—

Human toxicologists usually will answer questions about animal poisoning. There is no charge for this service.

SOME SOURCES OF INFORMATION ABOUT CANINE HEALTH

American Kennel Club (AKC)
5580 Centerview Drive
Raleigh, NC 27606
Customer Service: (919) 233-9767
info@akc.org

American Society for the Prevention of Cruelty to Animals (ASPCA)
441 East 92nd Street
New York, NY 10128
(212) 876-7700
(212) 348-3031
www.aspca.org/

American Veterinary Medical Association
1931 N. Meacham Road, Suite 100
Schaumburg, IL 60173-4360
(847) 925-8070 or (800) 248-AVMA
www.avma.org

Orthopedic Foundation for Animals (OFA)
2300 East Nifong Blvd.
Columbia, MO 65201-3856
(573) 442-0418
ofa@offa.org

Veterinary Medical Database/Canine Eye Registration Foundation (VMDB/CERF)
1248 Lynn Hall
Purdue University
West Lafayette, IN 47906
(765) 494-8179
yshenvet.purdue.edu

A FEW CATALOG SOURCES FOR CANINE HEALTH PRODUCTS

Write or call these companies for their most recent catalog.

Drs. Foster and Smith
2253 Air Park Road
P.O. Box 100
Rhinelander, WI 54501-0100
1-800-826-7206
www.drsfostersmith.com

Farnum Companies, Inc.
301 West Osborn
Phoenix, AZ 85013
1-800-825-2555
www.farnumpet.com

Jeffers Pet Catalog
P.O. Box 100
Dothan, AL 36320-0100
1-800-533-3377

New England Serum Company
P.O. Box 128
Topsfield, MA 01983-0228
1-800-637-3786

Pedigrees
1989 Transit Way, Box 905
Brockport, NY 14420-0905
1-800-548-4786

R. C. Steele
1989 Transit Way
P.O. Box 910
Brockport, NY 14420-0919
1-800-872-3733
www.rcsteele.com

INDEX

MY DOG'S MEDICAL HISTORY

Name: _____

Date of Birth: _____

Vaccination Record: _____

_____

_____

_____

Parasite Treatment: _____

_____

_____

_____

Surgery: _____

_____

_____

_____

Illnesses: _____

_____

_____

_____

OWNER'S NOTES

_____
_____
_____
_____
_____
_____
_____
_____
_____
_____
_____
_____
_____
_____
_____
_____
_____

OWNER'S NOTES

_____
_____
_____
_____
_____
_____
_____
_____
_____
_____
_____
_____
_____
_____
_____
_____
_____

OWNER'S NOTES

_____

_____

_____

_____

_____

_____

_____

_____

_____

_____

_____

_____

_____

_____

_____

_____

_____

_____

_____

OWNER'S NOTES

_____
_____
_____
_____
_____
_____
_____
_____
_____
_____
_____
_____
_____
_____
_____
_____
_____
_____
_____

OWNER'S NOTES

_____

_____

_____

_____

_____

_____

_____

_____

_____

_____

_____

_____

_____

_____

_____

_____

_____

_____